Carlos Martinez

No Great Wall

On The Continuities of the Chinese Revolution

The Publishing Press of
**THE MIDWESTERN MARX INSTITUTE FOR
MARXIST THEORY AND POLITICAL ANALYSIS**

Winter, 2022

www.midwesternmarx.com

Dubuque, IA/ Carbondale, IL USA

Midwestern Marx Publishing Press: Titles Published

1. Thomas Riggins. *Reading the Classical Texts of Marxism*, 2022.
2. Carlos L. Garrido. *Marxism and the Dialectical Materialist Worldview: An Anthology of Classical Marxist Texts on Dialectical Materialism*, 2022.
3. Thomas Riggins. *Eurocommunism: A Critical Reading of Santiago Carrillo and Eurocommunist Revisionism*, 2022.

Some Forthcoming Titles

1. Carlos L. Garrido and Noah Khrachvik. *Selected Works of Henry Winston.*
2. Thomas Riggins. *Christopher Caudwell and His Critics: A Study of Caudwell's Philosophy of Art and its Critical Responses.*
3. Edward Liger Smith. *What About Venezuela?: How Socialism Worked in Venezuela and Why the US Needs it Too.*
4. Yanis Iqbal. *Education in the Age of Neoliberal Dystopia.*
5. Noah Khrachvik. *What is to be Done... Like Now?*
6. Gabriel Rockhill, William Robinson, Salvador Rangel, Jennifer Ponce de León, Carlos Martinez, Carlos L. Garrido, Edward Smith, Noah Khrachvik, Thomas Riggins, Hilbourne Watson, et. al. *Against the Fake Left: Marxist Critiques of Contemporary Radicalisms.*

Table of Contents

No Great Wall: On the Continuities of the Chinese Revolution

Introduction

The Communist Party of China (CPC) was formed in July 1921. From that time up to the present day, it has led the Chinese Revolution – a revolution to eliminate feudalism, to regain China's national sovereignty, to end foreign domination of China, to build socialism, to create a better life for the Chinese people, and to contribute to a peaceful and prosperous future for humanity.

Some of these goals have already been achieved; others are ongoing. Thus the Chinese Revolution is a continuing process, and its basic political orientation remains the same.

Feudalism was dismantled in CPC-controlled territories from the early 1930s onwards, and throughout the country in the period immediately following the establishment of the People's Republic in 1949. Similarly, warlord rule was ended and a unified China essentially established in 1949; Hong Kong was returned to Chinese rule in 1997 and Macao in 1999. Only Taiwan continues to be governed separately and to serve foreign interests. And yet in a world system still principally defined by US hegemony, the imperialist threat remains – and is intensifying with the development of a US-led hybrid war against China. Therefore the project of protecting China's sovereignty and resisting imperialism continues. Similarly, the path to socialism is constantly evolving.

In the course of trying to build socialism in a vast semi-colonial, semi-feudal country, mistakes have certainly been made. The collected works of Marx and Lenin bubble over with profound ideas, but they contain no templates or formulae. Chinese Marxists have had to continuously engage in "concrete analysis of concrete conditions",[1] applying and developing socialist theory, creatively adapting it to an ever-changing material reality. In their foreword to Agnes Smedley's biography of Zhu De, *The Great Road*, Leo Huberman and Paul Sweezy wrote that the Chinese communists, "in the midst of their struggle for survival … have proceeded to evolve a more flexible and sophisticated theory which enriched Marxism by reflecting and absorbing the stubborn realities of the Chinese scene."[2]

As Liu Shaoqi, a prominent CPC leader until his denunciation during the Cultural Revolution, explained: "because of the distinctive peculiarities in China's social and historical development and her backwardness in science, it is a unique and difficult task to apply Marxism systematically to China and to transform it from its European form into a Chinese form… Many of these problems have never been solved or raised by the world's Marxists, for here in China the main section of the masses are not workers but peasants, and the fight is directed against foreign imperialist oppression and medieval survivals, and not against domestic capitalism."[3]

This work argues that, while the Chinese Revolution has taken numerous twists and turns, and while the CPC leadership has adopted different strategies at different times, there is a common thread running through modern Chinese history: of the CPC dedicating itself to navigating a path to socialism, development and independence, improving the lot of the Chinese people, and contributing to a peaceful and prosperous future for humanity.

Historical Background

The CPC was formed in response to a clear need for revolutionary leadership. The 1911 bourgeois revolution that had finally overthrown the Qing dynasty and established the Republic of China had come to a dead end, owing to the manoeuvring of the imperialist powers and their comprador agents. Most of the country was run by warlords. The feudal economy remained in place and the bulk of the population remained permanently on the brink of starvation, indebted to landlords. The various imperialist powers maintained their footholds, with Britain, the US, Japan and Germany competing for control of China's land and resources.

Young people in particular were searching for a path forward. "Youth organisations and study circles sprang up in great profusion", writes Israel Epstein,[4] including the New People's Study Society in Hunan, led by a certain Mao Zedong. A turning point came on 4 May 1919, when the students of Beijing marched on the government buildings in protest at the Treaty of Versailles, which legalised the Japanese seizure of Shandong province and rejected China's demands for the abolition of foreign spheres of influence and the withdrawal of foreign troops. The demonstrations caught the imagination of students, workers and radical intellectuals throughout the country. "The May 4 Movement was a climactic point of the Chinese revolution. It took place after, and was one of the results of, the October Revolution in Russia."[5] Han Suyin described the May 4 Movement as "a leap of consciousness, a radicalisation, which would determine the course of history."[6]

The CPC, formed two years later, was the first organisation to put forward the slogan 'Down with imperialism', recognising that China's weakness and backwardness were inherently bound up with foreign domination. Some relatively forward-thinking elements of the emerging capitalist class had hoped that the US or Japan might help China to establish itself as a modern capitalist power, but the communists recognised that this reflected a fundamental misunderstanding of the nature of imperialism. The major capitalist powers were compelled by the nature of their economic system to compete for control of China – a country offering an abundance of land, people, natural resources, and geostrategic advantage. Japan, the US, Britain, Germany and others wouldn't hesitate to support feudal warlords where it suited their interests; nor would they hesitate to suppress the Chinese people's desire for independence and progress. The CPC's anti-imperialist position quickly won it the support of a significant section of the population.

Soon after its formation, at its Third Congress in 1923, the CPC pushed for a united front with the Guomindang (GMD)[7], a revolutionary nationalist party set up by Sun Yat-sen in 1912 (the veteran politician and doctor Sun was elected as provisional president of the Republic of China following the overthrow of the Qing Dynasty). The idea of the united front was to construct an anti-imperialist alliance incorporating workers, peasants, intellectuals and the patriotic elements of the capitalist class, with a view to decisively ending feudalism, uniting the country under a single central government, and driving out the imperialist powers. Denied recognition or support by the West, the GMD was in the process of orienting towards the recently-formed Soviet Union, which had already demonstrated itself to be a supporter of Chinese sovereignty (the Bolsheviks had indicated their support for Sun Yat-sen as early as 1912[8] and, once in power, renounced all privileges in China granted to the tsarist regime). Recognising that the CPC would be more effective in mobilising the masses of the working class and peasantry, the GMD agreed to the CPC's proposal, and the CPC leadership took joint membership of both organisations.

This first united front started to fracture after the death in 1925 of Sun Yat-sen. The GMD's right wing gained the ascendancy under the leadership of Chiang Kai-shek (who would later go on to become the highly authoritarian leader of Taiwan from 1949 until his death in 1975). Chiang "believed that communism was inhuman and that, unless defeated, it would mean oppression for the Chinese people and the destruction of their traditional culture."[9] Fearing that the communists were gaining too much popular support, Chiang orchestrated a coup against them, in collaboration with the various foreign powers that had recognised in Chiang a potential partner in the pursuit of an 'acceptable' political conjuncture in China.

When, in April 1927, Shanghai was liberated from warlord control as the result of an insurrection of the local working class (led primarily by CPC forces), Chiang's forces won control of the city by means of a massacre of its liberators, killing an estimated 5,000 people. This marked the start of a several-year campaign of mass killings by Chiang's forces against communists and progressive workers. With CPC members formally ejected from the GMD and the united front dismantled, Chiang Kai-shek set up a new regime in Nanjing, under which "communism became a crime punishable by death."[10] The government focused its efforts not on resisting imperialism or uniting the country but on suppressing communists. Facing something close to physical annihilation, the membership of the CPC fell from 58,000 at the start of 1927 to 10,000 by the end of the year.

These disastrous events led the communists to a strategic reorientation. It was clear that a united front policy focused on the major urban centres was no longer a viable option. Meanwhile, "as every schoolboy knows, 80 per cent of China's population are peasants,"[11] and, as William Hinton writes in the preface to his classic account *Fanshen*, "without understanding the land question one cannot understand the Revolution in China."[12] The CPC was moving towards the development of a rural-based revolutionary movement.

Following a failed uprising in his native Hunan, Mao Zedong fled with his forces into the Jinggang mountains, in the border region of Jiangxi and Hunan provinces. This became the birthplace of the Chinese Red Army and the site of the first liberated territory. The Jiangxi Soviet expanded over the course of several years to incorporate parts of seven counties and a population of more than half a million.

Han Suyin notes that Mao Zedong "was the first in the party who abandoned the city orientation and devised a major strategy born from China's reality." The working class were a growing force, but constituted less than one percent of the population. "Mao saw that setting up rural bases, dedicated to the liberation of the peasantry from the oppression of landlordism, was the only way in which revolution would succeed."[13] Not only was the mass of the peasantry against feudal exploitation, but it could also understand the connection between foreign domination and domestic poverty. The period of foreign aggression from 1840 had led to wars and instability, much of the burden of which fell on the peasantry, which was expected to provide soldiers and sustenance. Any agricultural surplus from good harvest years was redirected to the state (or local warlord), leaving grain reserves empty and thus contributing to vast famines.

The CPC and Red Army grew in strength and experience during this time. Chiang Kai-shek's obsessive focus on eliminating communism led Mao and his comrades to develop a theory of guerrilla warfare that would prove decisive in the CPC's rise to power. However, China was rendered vulnerable to attack by Chiang's pacification programme. Even when the Japanese occupied Manchuria in September 1931, siphoning Manchukuo off as an 'independent' puppet state a year later, Chiang's clearly stated policy was: "Internal pacification first, before external resistance".

Between 1929 and 1934, Chiang's forces led a series of brutal encirclement campaigns in an attempt to bury the Jiangxi Soviet. After suffering a series of defeats at the hands of a highly motivated and skilled Red Army, the Guomindang mobilised warlord armies from around the country, organising a force of more than a million troops. The communists had no choice but to abandon the liberated territory and break the siege. This process became the Long March: the extraordinary year-long retreat to the North-West, covering over 9,000 kilometres and ending with the establishment of a revolutionary base area in Shaanxi. This area would serve as the centre of the CPC's operations until shortly before the formation of the People's Republic of China in 1949.

In the liberated territories, the communists led the creation of a new political economy in the countryside that – along with their determined struggle against Japanese militarism – would earn them the support of the broad masses of the peasantry. In his classic account *Red Star Over China*, Edgar Snow paints a vivid picture of life in the red base areas: "Land was redistributed and taxes were lightened. Collective enterprise was established on a wide scale…Unemployment, opium, prostitution, child slavery, and compulsory marriage were reported to be eliminated, and the living conditions of the workers and poor peasants in the peaceful areas greatly improved. Mass education made much progress in the stabilised soviets. In some counties the Reds attained a higher degree of literacy among the populace in three or four years than had been achieved anywhere else in rural China after centuries."[14]

Opium production was ended and replaced by food agriculture. Antiquated feudal practices such as foot-binding, infanticide and the keeping of slave girls were prohibited. Peng Dehuai, one of the top Red Army leaders and later the Defence Minister of the PRC, commented on the decisive importance of the CPC's progressive and popular policies in the liberated areas:

> "Only by implanting itself deeply in the hearts of the people, only by fulfilling the demands of the masses, only by consolidating a base in the peasant soviets, and only by sheltering in the shadow of the masses, can partisan warfare bring revolutionary victory… Tactics are important, but we could not exist if the majority of the people did not support us."[15]

By the mid 1930s, the Japanese armed forces were consolidating and expanding their occupation of Northeast China, aided and abetted by the Western powers, who were motivated by the idea of cooperating with Japan to attack the Soviet Union. Chiang Kai-shek's position was becoming untenable. He granted concession after concession to the Japanese, but he could no longer justify his refusal to defend China's national sovereignty. In July 1937, Japanese forces marched out of their puppet state of Manchukuo, going on to occupy Beijing and Shanghai.

In this context, more progressive elements within the GMD took the initiative, detaining Chiang in the northwestern city of Xi'an and forcing him to agree to cooperate with the CPC against Japanese occupation. Thus was formed the Second United Front. The red base at Yan'an (Shaanxi) was recognised as a provincial government and the CPC was legalised; the Red Army was re-designated as the Eighth Route Army.

New Democracy

In the period of the Second United Front, the CPC won enormous prestige for its leadership of the national defence efforts and for its commitment to improving the lives of the population in the territories under its control. Yan'an became a pole of attraction for revolutionary and progressive youth throughout the country. British academic Graham Hutchings writes that "Yan'an seemed to stand for a new type of society. Visitors, foreign and Chinese, found it brimming with purpose, equality and hope. Many students and intellectuals chose to leave areas under the control of a central government they felt lacked a sense of justice, as well as the will to confront the national enemy, for life in the border regions and the communist or 'progressive' camp."[16]

It was increasingly clear that the communists were the most cohesive, committed and competent political force in China; the only political party with the potential to restore China's sovereignty, unity and dignity. Mao and the CPC leadership took the time to theorise the type of society they were trying to build; what the substance of their revolution was. The results of these debates and discussions are synthesised in Mao's 1940 pamphlet *On New Democracy*, which describes the Chinese Revolution as necessarily having two stages: "first of New Democracy and then of socialism."[17]

New Democracy was not to be a socialist society, but a "democratic republic under the joint dictatorship of all anti-imperialist and anti-feudal people led by the proletariat." Extending a friendly hand to patriotic non-communist forces, Mao invoked the spirit of Sun Yat-sen, calling for "a republic of the genuinely revolutionary new Three People's Principles with their Three Great Policies." (The *Three People's Principles* were – approximately – nationalism, people's government, and social welfare; the *Three Great Policies* were alliance with the Soviet

Union, alliance with the CPC, and support for the workers and peasants).

The key elements of this stage of the revolution were to defeat imperialism and to establish independence, as an essential step on the road to the longer-term goal of building socialism. How long would this stage last? It would "need quite a long time and cannot be accomplished overnight. We are not utopians and cannot divorce ourselves from the actual conditions confronting us."[18]

Such a society would not be a dictatorship of the proletariat; that is, the working class would not exercise exclusive political control. Rather, political power would be shared by all the anti-imperialist classes: the working class, the peasantry, the petty bourgeoisie and the national bourgeoisie (ie those elements of the capitalist class that stood against foreign domination).

In economic terms, New Democracy would include elements of both socialism and capitalism. "The state enterprises will be of a socialist character and will constitute the leading force in the whole national economy, but the republic will neither confiscate capitalist private property in general nor forbid the development of such capitalist production as does not 'dominate the livelihood of the people', for China's economy is still very backward." Land reform would be carried out, and the activities of private capital would be subjected to heavy regulation.

In conversation with Edgar Snow, Mao envisaged China taking its place within an ever-more globalised world – perhaps anticipating the 'opening up' of four decades later: "When China really wins her independence, then legitimate foreign trading interests will enjoy more opportunities than ever before. The power of production and consumption of 450 million people is not a matter that can remain the exclusive interest of the Chinese, but one that must engage the many nations. Our millions of people, once really emancipated, with their great latent productive possibilities freed for creative activity in every field, can help improve the economy as well as raise the cultural level of the whole world."[19]

Following Japan's defeat in 1945, the CPC and GMD attempted to negotiate a post-war government alliance. However, the agreement forged in Chongqing in October 1945 fell apart as Chiang's forces continued their military attacks on the CPC-controlled areas. A bitter four-year civil war ensued, resulting in the communists' victory, Chiang Kai-shek's flight to Taiwan, and the establishment of the People's Republic of China on 1 October 1949. The newly-installed government, led by the CPC, attempted to build the type of society described in *On New Democracy*. Its governance was based on the Common Programme – an interim constitution drawn up by the Chinese People's Political Consultative Conference (a united front body created by the CPC), with 662 delegates representing 45 different organisations. The Common Programme did not call for the immediate establishment of a socialist society, and it promised to encourage private business. As Mao had written earlier in the year, "our present policy is to regulate capitalism and not to destroy it."[20] Patriotic capitalists were invited to participate in government.

The most important immediate economic change was the comprehensive dismantling of feudalism: the abolition of the rural class system and the distribution of land to the peasantry (a process already well underway in the areas under CPC control). Land reform resulted in a large agricultural surplus which, along with Soviet support, created the conditions for a rapid state-led industrialisation. Hutchings notes that "dramatic improvements in life expectancy and literacy rates and increases in living standards accompanied the appearance of factories, roads, railways and bridges across the country."[21] Along with this came an unprecedented shift in the status of women, who had suffered every oppression and indignity under feudalism. Via a system of "barefoot doctors", basic medical care was made available to the peasantry. "As a consequence, fertility rose, infant mortality declined, life expectancy began to climb, and the population stabilised and then grew for the first time since the Japanese invasion of 1937."[22]

The New Democracy period only lasted a few years. By 1954, the government was promoting collectivisation in the countryside and shifting private production into state hands. By the time of the Great Leap Forward in 1958, there was no more talk of a slow and cautious road to socialism; the plan now was to "surpass Britain and catch up to America" within 15 years.

The reasons for moving on from New Democracy are complex and contested, and reflect a shifting global political environment. The CPC had envisaged – or at least hoped for – mutually beneficial relations with the West, as is hinted at in the quote above that "legitimate foreign trading interests will enjoy more opportunities than ever before". However, by the time of the founding of the PRC, the Cold War was already in full swing. After the defeat of Japan in 1945, and with the outbreak of civil war between the communists and the nationalists, the US came down on the side of the latter, on the basis that Chiang understood the civil war to be "an integral part of the worldwide conflict between communism and capitalism"[23] and was resolutely on the side of capitalism.

The US made its hostility to the People's Republic manifestly clear from early on. The US involvement in the Korean War, starting in June 1950, was to no small degree connected to "the West's determination … to 'contain' revolutionary China."[24] The genocidal force directed against the Korean people – including the repeated threat of nuclear warfare – was also a warning to China's communists (although the warning was returned with interest, when hundreds of thousands of Chinese volunteers joined hands with their Korean brothers and sisters, rapidly pushing the US-led troops back to the 38th parallel and forcing an effective stalemate). Soon after the arrival of US troops in Korea, US President Truman announced that his government would act to prevent Taiwan's incorporation into the PRC, since this would constitute "a threat to the security of the Pacific area and to United States forces performing their lawful and necessary functions in that area."[25] Truman ordered the Seventh Fleet of the US Navy into the Taiwan Strait in order to prevent China from occupying it (such, incidentally, are the imperialist origins of the notion of Taiwanese independence). Along with these acts of physical aggression, the US imposed a total embargo on China, depriving the country of various important materials required for reconstruction.

The dangerously hostile external environment made New Democracy less viable. There are parallels here with the Soviet abandonment of the New Economic Policy (NEP) in 1929. Much like New Democracy, the NEP had consisted of a mixed economy, with private business encouraged in order to increase production and enhance productivity. Introduced in 1921, the NEP proved highly successful, allowing the Soviet Union to recover economically from war whilst minimising internal class conflict. By the end of the decade, however, new external dangers were emerging and it became clear to the Soviet leadership that the imperialist powers were starting to mobilise for war. From 1929 the Soviet economy shifted to something like a wartime basis, with near-total centralisation, total state ownership of industry, collectivisation of agriculture, and a major focus on heavy industry and military production.

Similarly in China in the mid-1950s, the shifting regional situation contributed to an economic and political shift. Beyond that, there was undoubtedly a subjective factor of the CPC leadership wanting to accelerate the journey to socialism – to "accomplish socialist industrialisation and socialist transformation in fifteen years or a little longer", as Mao put it in 1953.[26] With the death of Stalin in March 1953 and the gradual deterioration of relations between the CPC and the new Soviet leadership under Nikita Khrushchev, the Chinese came to feel that the Soviets were abandoning the path of revolutionary struggle and that responsibility for blazing a trail in the construction of socialism had fallen to China. To move from a position of economic and scientific backwardness to becoming an advanced socialist power would require nothing less than a great leap.

Mao as Monster?

To this day, the most popular method for casually denigrating the People's Republic of China and the record of the CPC is to cite the alleged crimes of Mao Zedong who, from the early 1930s until his death in 1976, was generally recognised as the top leader of the Chinese Revolution. If the CPC was so dedicated to improving the lot of the Chinese people, why did it engage in such disastrous campaigns as the Great Leap Forward and the Cultural Revolution?

The Great Leap Forward, launched in 1958, was an ambitious programme designed to achieve rapid industrialisation and collectivisation; to fast-track the construction of socialism and allow China to make a final break with centuries-old underdevelopment and poverty; in Mao's words, to "close the gap between China and the US within five years, and to ultimately surpass the US within seven years".[27] In its economic strategy, it represented "a rejection of plodding Soviet-style urban industrialisation,"[28] reflecting the early stages of the Sino-Soviet split. The Chinese were worried that the Khrushchev leadership in Moscow was narrowly focused on the avoidance of conflict with the imperialist powers, and that its support to China and the other socialist countries would be sacrificed at the altar of 'peaceful coexistence'. Hence China would have to rely on its own resources.

For all its shortcomings, the core of the GLF was pithily described by Indian Marxist Vijay Prashad as an "attempt to bring small-scale industry to rural areas."[29] Mao considered the countryside would once again become the "true source for revolutionary social transformation" and "the main arena where the struggle to achieve socialism and communism will be determined."[30] Agricultural collectivisation was fast-tracked, and there was a broad appeal to the revolutionary spirit of the masses. Ji Chaozhu (at the time an interpreter for the Ministry of Foreign Affairs and later China's ambassador to the UK (1987-91)) notes in his memoirs: "The peasants were left with small plots of their own, for subsistence farming only. All other activity was for the communal good, to be shared equally. Cadres were to join the peasants in the fields, factories, and construction sites. Even Mao made an appearance at a dam-building project to have his picture taken with a shovel in hand."[31]

The GLF was not overall a success. Liu Mingfu writes that "the Great Leap Forward did not realise the goal of surpassing the UK and US. It actually brought China's economy to a standstill and then recession. It caused a large number of unnatural deaths and pushed China's global share of GDP from 5.46% in 1957 to 4.01% in 1962, lower than its share of 4.59% in 1950."[32]

The disruption to the basic economic structure of society combined with the sudden withdrawal of Soviet experts in 1960 and a series of terrible droughts and floods to produce poor harvests. Meanwhile, with millions of peasants drafted into the cities to work in factories, "no one was available to reap and to thresh."[33] The historian Alexander Pantsov writes that the "battle for steel had diverted the Chinese leadership's attention from the grain problem, and the task of harvesting rice and other grain had fallen on the shoulders of women, old men, and children… A shortage of grain developed, and Mao gave the command to decrease the pace of the Great Leap."[34] Ji Chaozhu observes that "malnutrition leading to edema was common in many areas, and deaths among the rural population increased."[35]

Certain of the GLF's goals were achieved – most notably the irrigation of arable land. However, it didn't achieve its overall objective, and the disruption it caused contributed to a deepening of poverty and malnutrition. It was called off in 1962. It remains a highly controversial topic in Chinese history. For anticommunists, the GLF provides incontrovertible proof of the monstrous, murderous nature of the CPC – and Mao Zedong in particular. Western bourgeois historians seem to have settled on a figure of 30 million for the estimated number of lives lost in famine resulting from the Great Leap. On the basis of a rigorous statistical analysis, Indian economist Utsa Patnaik concludes that China's death rate rose from 12 per thousand in 1958 (a historically low figure resulting from land reform and the extension of basic medical services throughout the country) to a peak of 25.4 per thousand in 1960. "If we take the remarkably low death rate of 12 per thousand that China had achieved by 1958 as the benchmark, and calculate the deaths in excess of this over the period 1959 to 1961, it totals 11.5 million. This is the maximal estimate of possible 'famine deaths.'"[36]

Patnaik observes that even the peak death rate in 1960 "was little different from India's 24.8 death rate in the same year, which was considered quite normal and attracted no criticism." This is an important point. Malnutrition was at that time a scourge throughout the developing world (sadly it remains so in some parts of the planet). China's history is rife with terrible famines, including in 1907, 1928 and 1942. It is only in the modern era, under the leadership of precisely that 'monstrous' CPC, that malnutrition has become a thing of the past in China.

In other words, the failure of the GLF has been cynically manipulated by bourgeois academics to denigrate the entire history of the Chinese Revolution. The GLF was not some outrageous crime against humanity; it was a legitimate attempt to accelerate the building of a prosperous and advanced socialist society. It turned out not to be successful and was therefore dropped.

In the aftermath of the GLF, Mao's more radical wing of the CPC leadership became somewhat marginalised, and the initiative fell to those wanting to prioritise social stability and economic growth over ongoing class struggle. Principal among these were Liu Shaoqi (head of state of the PRC, widely considered to be Mao's successor) and Vice Premier Deng Xiaoping. Liu, Deng, Chen Yun and Zhou Enlai put forward the concept of the *Four Modernisations* (in agriculture, industry, defence, and science and technology) which would come to constitute a cornerstone of post-Mao economic policy.

In the years that followed, Mao and a group of his close comrades began to worry that the deprioritisation of class struggle reflected an anti-revolutionary 'revisionist' trend that could ultimately lead to capitalist restoration. As Mao saw it, revisionist elements were able to rely on the support of the intelligentsia – particularly teachers and academics – who, themselves coming largely from non-working class backgrounds, were promoting capitalist and feudal values among young people. It was necessary to "exterminate the roots of revisionism" and "struggle against those in power in the party who were taking the capitalist road."[37]

The Cultural Revolution started in 1966 as a mass movement of university and school students, incited and encouraged by Mao and others on the left of the leadership. Student groups formed in Beijing calling themselves Red Guards and taking up Mao's call to "thoroughly criticise and repudiate the reactionary bourgeois ideas in the sphere of academic work, education, journalism, literature and art".[38] The students produced 'big-character posters' (*dazibao*) setting out their analysis against, and making their demands of, anti-revolutionary bourgeois elements in authority. Mao was enthusiastic, writing the students in support of their initiative: "I will give enthusiastic support to all who take an attitude similar to yours in the Cultural Revolution movement."[39] He produced his own *dazibao* calling on the revolutionary masses to "Bombard the Headquarters" – that is, to rise up against the reformers and "bourgeois elements" in the party.

These developments were synthesised by the CPC Central Committee, which in August 1966 adopted its *Decision Concerning the Great Proletarian Cultural Revolution*. "Although the bourgeoisie has been overthrown, it is still trying to use the old ideas, culture, customs and habits of the exploiting classes to corrupt the masses, capture their minds and endeavour to stage a comeback. The proletariat must do the exact opposite: it must meet head-on every challenge of the bourgeoisie in the ideological field and use the new ideas, culture, customs and habits of the proletariat to change the mental outlook of the whole of society. At present, our objective is to struggle against and overthrow those persons in authority who are taking the capitalist road, to criticise and repudiate the reactionary bourgeois academic 'authorities' and the ideology of the bourgeoisie and all other exploiting classes and to transform education, literature and art and all other parts of the superstructure not in correspondence with the socialist economic base, so as to facilitate the consolidation and development of the socialist system."[40]

Thus the aims of the Cultural Revolution were to stimulate a mass struggle against the supposedly revisionist and capitalist restorationist elements in the party; to put a stop to the hegemony of bourgeois ideas in the realms of education and culture; and to entrench a new culture – socialist, collectivist, modern. The Cultural Revolution also marked a further escalation of the Sino-Soviet split, as the revisionist illness was considered to have a Soviet etiology (Liu Shaoqi, previously considered as Mao's successor and now the principal target of the radicals, was labelled *China's Khrushchev*). Li Mingjiang notes that, "throughout the Cultural Revolution, the Soviet Union was systematically demonised. Sino-Soviet hostilities reached an unprecedented level, as exemplified by Mao's designation of Moscow as China's primary enemy."[41]

Han Suyin describes the chaotic atmosphere of the early days of the Cultural Revolution: "Extensive democracy. Great criticism. Wall posters everywhere. Absolute freedom to travel. Freedom to form revolutionary exchanges. These were the rights and freedoms given to the Red Guards, and no wonder it went to their heads and very soon became total licence." In August 1966, "the simmering Cultural Revolution exploded in a maelstrom of violence… Mao had not reckoned that he would lose control of the havoc he had launched."[42]

There was widespread disruption. Universities were closed. "Red Guards occupied and ransacked the Foreign Ministry, while most ambassadors were recalled to Beijing for political education. The British embassy was attacked, and the Soviet embassy was laid under siege by youthful Maoists for several months."[43]

Many of those accused by the Cultural Revolution Group (CRG, a body of the CPC initially reporting to the Politburo Standing Committee but becoming the de facto centre of power) suffered horrible fates. Posters appeared with the slogan "Down with Liu Shaoqi! Down with Deng Xiaoping! Hold high the great red banner of Mao Zedong Thought." Liu's books were burned in Tiananmen Square – "they were declared to be poisonous weeds, yet they had been a mainstay of the theoretical construct which in Yen'an in 1945-47 had brought Mao to power."[44] He was expelled from all positions and arrested. "Liu had been repeatedly tortured and interrogated, confined to an unheated cell, and denied medical care. He died in November 1969, his remains surreptitiously cremated under a false name. His death was kept from his wife for three years, and from the public for a decade."[45]

Peng Dehuai, former Defence Minister and the leader of the Chinese People's Volunteer Army's operations in the Korean War, had been forced into retirement in 1959 after criticising the Great Leap Forward. Jiang Qing – Mao's wife, and a leading figure in the CRG – sent Red Guards to Sichuan, where Peng was living. "A band of thugs burst into his house, seized him, and brought him to the capital, where he was thrown into prison. Peng was tortured and beaten more than a hundred times, his ribs were broken, his face maimed, and his lungs damaged. He was repeatedly dragged to criticism and struggle meetings."[46] He died in a prison hospital in 1974.

Even Premier Zhou Enlai, unfailingly loyal in spite of his quiet horror at the CRG's extremism, didn't escape unscathed: in November 1966, according to Han Suyin, he had a heart attack after 22 hours of being surrounded and shouted at by Red Guards.

Although Mao had only intended it to last for a few months, the Cultural Revolution only came to its conclusion shortly before Mao's death in 1976, albeit with varying intensity – realising that the situation was getting out of control, in 1967 Mao called on the army to help establish order and re-organise production. However, the Cultural Revolution flared up again with the ascendancy of the 'Gang of Four' from 1972.

Historians in the capitalist countries tend to present the Cultural Revolution in the most facile and vacuous terms. To them, it was simply the quintessential example of Mao's obsessive love of violence and power; just another episode in the long story of communist authoritarianism. But psychopathology is rarely the principal driving force of history. In reality, the Cultural Revolution was a radical mass movement; millions of young people were inspired by the idea of moving faster towards socialism, of putting an end to feudal traditions, of creating a more egalitarian society, of fighting bureaucracy, of preventing the emergence of a capitalist class, of empowering workers and peasants, of making their contribution to a global socialist revolution, of building a proud socialist culture unfettered by thousands of years of Confucian tradition. They wanted a fast track to a socialist future. They were inspired by Mao and his allies, who were in turn inspired by them.

Such a movement can get out of control easily enough, and it did. Mao can't be considered culpable for every excess, every act of violence, every absurd statement (indeed he intervened at several points to rein it in), but he was broadly supportive of the movement and ultimately did the most to further its aims. Mao had enormous personal influence – not solely powers granted by the party or state constitutions, but an authority that came from being the chief architect of a revolutionary process that had transformed hundreds of millions of people's lives for the better. He was as Lenin was to the Soviet people, as Fidel Castro remains to the Cuban people. Even when he made mistakes, these mistakes were liable to be embraced by millions of people. Han Suyin comments that "Mao was prone to making contradictory remarks, but each remark had the force of an edict."[47]

The Cultural Revolution is now widely understood in China to have been misguided. It was "the most severe setback … suffered by the Party, the state and the people since the founding of the People's Republic."[48] The political assumptions of the movement – that the party was becoming dominated by counter-revolutionaries and capitalist-roaders; that the capitalist-roaders in the party would have to be overthrown by the masses; that continuous revolution would be required in order to stay on the road to socialism – were explicitly rejected by the post-Mao leadership of the CPC, which pointed out that "the 'capitalist-roaders' overthrown … were leading cadres of Party and government organisations at all levels, who formed the core force of the socialist cause."[49] Historian Rebecca Karl posits that this post-Mao leadership in fact benefitted from the Cultural Revolution, in the sense that it became "the saviour of China from chaos."[50]

Unquestionably the turmoil of the Cultural Revolution impeded the country's development and brought awful tragedy to a significant number of people. What so many historians operating in a capitalist framework fail to understand is why, in spite of the chaos and violence of the Cultural Revolution, Mao is still revered in China. For the Chinese people, the bottom line is that his errors were "the errors of a great proletarian revolutionary."[51]

It was the CPC, led by Mao and on the basis of a political strategy principally devised by him, that China was liberated from foreign rule; that the country was unified; that feudalism was dismantled; that land was distributed to the peasants; that the country was industrialised; that a path to women's liberation was forged. British academic John Ross points out that, "in the 27 years between the establishment of the People's Republic of China in 1949 and the death of Mao Zedong in 1976, life expectancy in China increased by 31 years – or over a year per chronological year... China's rate of increase of life expectancy in the three decades after 1949 was the fastest ever recorded in a major country in human history."[52]

The excesses and errors associated with the last years of Mao's life have to contextualised within this overall picture of unprecedented, transformative progress for the Chinese people. The pre-revolution literacy rate in China was less than 20 percent. By the time Mao died, it was around 93 percent. China's population had remained stagnant between 400 and 500 million for a hundred years or so up to 1949. By the time Mao died, it had reached 900 million. A thriving culture of literature, music, theatre and art grew up that was accessible to the masses of the people. Land was irrigated. Famine became a thing of the past. Universal healthcare was established. China – after a century of foreign domination – maintained its sovereignty and developed the means to defend itself from imperialist attack.

Hence the *Mao as monster* narrative has little resonance in China. As Deng Xiaoping himself put it, "without Mao's outstanding leadership, the Chinese revolution would still not have triumphed even today. In that case, the people of all our nationalities would still be suffering under the reactionary rule of imperialism, feudalism and bureaucrat-capitalism."[53] Furthermore, even the mistakes were not the product of the deranged imagination of a tyrant but, rather, creative attempts to respond to an incredibly complex and evolving set of circumstances. They were errors carried out in the cause of exploring a path to socialism – a historically novel process inevitably involving risk and experimentation.

Reform and Opening Up: The Great Betrayal?

From 1978, the post-Mao Chinese leadership embarked on a process of 'reform and opening up' – gradually introducing market mechanisms to the economy, allowing elements of private property, and encouraging investment from the capitalist world. This programme of *socialism with Chinese characteristics* posited that, while China had established a socialist society, it would remain for some time in the primary stage of socialism, during which period it was necessary to develop a socialist market economy – combining planning, the development of a mixed economy and the profit motive – with a view to maximising the development of the productive forces.

Deng Xiaoping, who had been one of the most prominent targets of the Cultural Revolution and who had risen to become de facto leader of the CPC from 1978, theorised reform and opening up in the following terms: "Marxism attaches utmost importance to developing the productive forces… [The advance towards communism] calls for highly developed productive forces and an overwhelming abundance of material wealth. Therefore, the fundamental task for the socialist stage is to develop the productive forces. The superiority of the socialist system is demonstrated, in the final analysis, by faster and greater development of those forces than under the capitalist system. As they develop, the people's material and cultural life will constantly improve… Socialism means eliminating poverty. Pauperism is not socialism, still less communism."[54]

Was this the moment the CPC gave up on its commitment to Marxism? Such is the belief of many. For supporters of capitalism, the idea that China 'ascended' to capitalism from 1978 onwards is a validation of their own ideology; China was socialist and poor, and then became capitalist and rich. This view is near-universal among mainstream economists. Even the well-known Keynesian Jeffrey Sachs, who is both politically progressive and friendly towards China, considers that the key turning point in Chinese history was not 1949 but 1978: "After nearly 140 years of economic and social strife, marked by foreign incursions, domestic rebellions, civil wars, and internal policy blunders of historic dimensions, China settled down after 1978 to stable, open, market-based production and trade."[55]

On the other hand, for many on the left (particularly in the West), 1978 marked a turning point in the wrong direction – away from socialism, away from the cause of the working class and peasantry. The introduction of private profit, the decollectivisation of agriculture, the appearance of multinational companies and the rise of Western influence: these added up to a historic betrayal and an end to the Chinese Revolution.

The consensus view within the CPC is that socialism with Chinese characteristics is a strategy aimed at strengthening socialism, improving the lives of the Chinese people, and consolidating China's sovereignty. Although China had taken incredible steps forward since 1949, China in 1978 remained backward in many ways. The bulk of the population lived a very precarious existence, many without access to modern energy and safe water. China's per capita income was $210. Food production, and consequently average food consumption, was insufficient. "An estimated 30 percent of rural residents, about 250 million, lived below the poverty line, relying on small loans for production and state grants for food."[56] The low per capita income figure is deceptive in the sense that the poor in China had secure access to land and housing – by which measure they were doing much better than most of their counterparts in the developing world; nonetheless the vast majority were genuinely poor.

Meanwhile the capitalist world was making major advances in science and technology, and the gap in living standards between China and its neighbours was growing sufficiently wide as to threaten the legitimacy of the CPC government. Chinese economist Justin Yifu Lin notes that, at the time of the founding of the PRC, there was only a relatively small per capita income gap between China and its East Asian neighbours. "But by 1978 Japan had basically caught up with the United States, and South Korea and Taiwan, China, had narrowed the income gap with developed countries. China, although boasting a complete industrial system, an atomic bomb, and a man-made satellite, had a standard of living a far cry from that of the developed world."[57]

In Guangdong, the southern province bordering Hong Kong, many were fleeing because, in the words of Hua Guofeng (Mao's chosen successor as head of the CPC), "Hong Kong and Macao were wealthy and the PRC was poor." The leadership simply decided to "change the situation and make the PRC wealthy."[58]

Opening up to foreign capital, learning from foreign technology, and integrating into the global market would allow for a faster development of the productive forces. Export manufacturing would allow China to build up sufficient hard currency to acquire technology from rich countries and improve productivity. Foreign capital would be attracted by China's virtually limitless pool of literate and diligent workers.

All this was highly unorthodox compared to the experience of the socialist world up to that point (with some partial exceptions, such as Yugoslavia and Hungary). Deng Xiaoping's strong belief was that, unless the government delivered on a significant improvement in people's standard of living, the entire socialist project would lose its legitimacy and therefore be in peril. Assessing that China was around 20 years behind the advanced countries in science and technology, he stated: "When a backward country is trying to build socialism, it is natural that during the long initial period its productive forces will not be up to the level of those in developed capitalist countries and that it will not be able to eliminate poverty completely. Accordingly, in building socialism we must do all we can to develop the productive forces and gradually eliminate poverty, constantly raising the people's living standards… If we don't do everything possible to increase production, how can we expand the economy? How can we demonstrate the superiority of socialism and communism? We have been making revolution for several decades and have been building socialism for more than three. Nevertheless, by 1978 the average monthly salary for our workers was still only 45 yuan, and most of our rural areas were still mired in poverty. Can this be called the superiority of socialism?"[59]

Interestingly, this sentiment contains echoes of Mao in 1949: "If we are ignorant in production, cannot grasp production work quickly … so as to improve the livelihood of workers first and then that of other ordinary people, we shall certainly not be able to maintain our political power: we shall lose our position and we shall fail."[60]

Marx wrote in volume 3 of *Capital* that "the development of the productive forces of social labour is capital's historic mission and justification. For that very reason, it unwittingly creates the material conditions for a higher form of production."[61] The vision of the CPC leadership was to replace "unwittingly" with "purposefully": using capital, within strict limits and under heavy regulation, to bring China into the modern world.

Rather than selling out to capitalism, *reform and opening up* is better understood as a return to the policies of the New Democracy period. The CPC has always been adamant that what China is building is socialism, not capitalism – "it is for the realisation of communism that we have struggled for so many years… It was for the realisation of this ideal that countless people laid down their lives."[62] The basic guiding ideology of the CPC has not changed in its century of existence, as was summed up succinctly by Xi Jinping: "Both history and reality have shown us that only socialism can save China and only socialism with Chinese characteristics can bring development to China."[63]

In borrowing certain techniques and mechanisms from capitalism, China is following a logic devised by the Bolsheviks during the New Economic Policy, using markets and investment to stimulate economic activity, whilst maintaining Communist Party rule and refusing to allow the capitalist class to dominate political power. As Lenin put it in 1921: "We must not be afraid of the growth of the petty bourgeoisie and small capital. What we must fear is protracted starvation, want and food shortage, which create the danger that the working class will be utterly exhausted and will give way to petty-bourgeois vacillation and despair. This is a much more terrible prospect."[64]

Modern China has gone much further than the NEP, in the sense that private property is not limited to "the petty bourgeoisie and small capital"; there are some extremely wealthy individuals and companies controlling vast sums of capital. And yet their political status is essentially the same as it was in the early days of the PRC; their existence as a class is predicated on their acceptance of the overall socialist programme and trajectory of the country. As long as they are helping China to develop, they are tolerated. Even in 1957, with socialist construction in full swing, Mao considered that "the contradiction between the working class and the national bourgeoisie comes under the category of contradictions among the people... In the concrete conditions of China, this antagonistic contradiction between the two classes, if properly handled, can be transformed into a non-antagonistic one and be resolved by peaceful methods."[65]

The reform strategy has been undeniably successful in terms of alleviating poverty and modernising the country. Economist Arthur Kroeber notes that workers' wages have increased continuously, pointing out that, in 1994, a Chinese factory worker could expect to earn a quarter of what their counterpart in Thailand was earning; just 14 years later, the Chinese worker was earning 25 percent more than the Thai worker.[66] Jude Woodward writes that per capita income in China doubled in the decade from 1980, "whereas it took Britain six decades to achieve the same after the Industrial Revolution in the late eighteenth century and America five decades after the Civil War."[67]

The combination of planning and ever-rising productivity has created a vast surplus, which has been used partly to "orchestrate a massive, sustained programme of infrastructure construction, including roads, railways, ports, airports, dams, electricity generation and distribution facilities, telecommunications, water and sewage systems, and housing, on a proportional scale far exceeding that of comparable developing countries, such as India, Indonesia, Pakistan and Bangladesh."[68]

The fundamental difference between the Chinese system and capitalism is that, with capital in control, it would not be possible to prioritise the needs of the working class and peasantry; China would not have been able to achieve the largest-scale poverty alleviation in history. Deng understood this: "Ours is an economically backward country with a population of one billion. If we took the capitalist road, a small number of people in certain areas would quickly grow rich, and a new bourgeoisie would emerge along with a number of millionaires — all of these people amounting to less than one per cent of the population — while the overwhelming majority of the people would remain in poverty, scarcely able to feed and clothe themselves. Only the socialist system can eradicate poverty."[69]

In adapting its strategy in accordance with new realities and a sober assessment of the past, the CPC was following the same principle it had always stood for: to seek truth from facts and to develop a reciprocal relationship between theory and practice. In Mao's words, "the only yardstick of truth is the revolutionary practice of millions of people."[70] The CPC's experience in practice was that "having a totally planned economy hampers the development of the productive forces to a certain extent."[71] Its leaders therefore conjectured that a combination of planning and markets would "liberate the productive forces and speed up economic growth." This hypothesis has been proven correct by material reality. As John Ross puts it, "China's extraordinary success during reform and opening up was based on adherence to Marxist theory and is the largest possible scale vindication of the Marxism in the framework of which reform and opening up was developed."[72]

No Great Wall

Reform and opening up wasn't purely a correction of earlier mistakes; it was also a response to changing objective circumstances; specifically, a more favourable international environment resulting from the restoration of China's seat at the United Nations (1971) and the rapprochement between China and the US. Thomas Orlik, chief economist at Bloomberg Economics, correctly observes that, "when Deng Xiaoping launched the reform and opening process, friendly relations with the United States provided the crucial underpinning. The path for Chinese goods to enter global markets was open."[73] So too was the door for foreign capital, technology, and expertise to enter China – first from Hong Kong and Japan, then the West. Zhou Enlai reportedly commented at the time of then-US Secretary of State Henry Kissinger's historic visit to Beijing in 1971 that "only America can help China to modernise."[74] Even allowing for Zhou's legendary diplomatic eloquence, this statement nevertheless contains an important kernel of truth.

Mao and Zhou had seen engagement with the US as a way to break China's isolation. The US leadership saw engagement with China as a way to perpetuate and exacerbate the division between China and the Soviet Union. (Everyone was triangulating; for its part, the Soviet leadership was hoping to work with the US to undermine and destabilise China.[75]) Regardless of the complex set of intentions, one key outcome of the US-China rapprochement in the early 1970s was that a favourable external environment was created in which a policy of 'opening up' could feasibly be pursued.

Deng was also not the first to recognise that the productive forces were undergoing historic changes in the West and that China would have to catch up. Zhou Enlai noted that "new developments in science are bringing humanity to a new technological and industrial revolution... we must conquer these new heights in science to reach advanced world standards."[76] Indeed it was Zhou that first conceptualised the *Four Modernisations* that Deng made the cornerstone of his strategy. Zhou talked in January 1975 – during his last major speech – of the urgent need to take advantage of the more peaceful and stable international context and "accomplish the comprehensive modernisation of agriculture, industry, national defence and science and technology before the end of the century, so that our national economy will be advancing in the front ranks of the world."[77]

The economic take-off of the post-1978 period "would not have been possible without the economic, political and social foundations that had been built up in the preceding period", in the words of the late Egyptian Marxist Samir Amin.[78] Even with the disruption caused by the Cultural Revolution, the early period of socialist construction achieved "progress on a scale which old China could not achieve in hundreds or even thousands of years."[79] This is widely understood within China. Prominent economist Hu Angang writes that, by 1978, all children received an education, adult illiteracy had fallen from 80 percent to 33 percent, and basic healthcare was available to everyone. Industry had been built up from almost nothing. Meanwhile, "China succeeded in feeding one-fifth of the world's population with only 7 percent of the world's arable land and 6.5 percent of its water. China's pre-1978 social and economic development cannot be underestimated."[80] This can be usefully compared with the same time period in India, which following independence from the British Empire in 1947 was in a similarly parlous state, with a life expectancy of 32. At the end of the pre-reform period in China, ie 1978, India's life expectancy had increased to 55, while China's had increased to 67. As John Ross elucidates, "this sharply growing difference was not because India had a bad record – as an increase of 22 years in life expectancy over a 31-year period graphically shows. It is simply that China's performance was sensational – life expectancy increasing by 32 years in a 29-year chronological period."[81]

Xi Jinping has observed that, although the two major phases of the People's Republic of China are different in many ways, "they are by no means separated from or opposed to each other. We should neither negate the pre-reform phase in comparison with the post-reform phase, nor the converse."[82]

The two major phases are both consistent with the CPC's guiding philosophy and raison d'être. Both have played an invaluable role in China's continuing transformation from a divided, war-torn, backward and phenomenally poor country in which "approximately one of every three children died within the first year of birth"[83] to a unified, peaceful, advanced and increasingly prosperous country which is blazing a trail towards a more developed socialism.

In each stage of its existence, the CPC has sought to creatively apply and develop Marxism according to the prevailing concrete circumstances; always seeking to safeguard China's sovereignty, maintain peace, and build prosperity for the masses of the people. Through many twists and turns, this has been a constant of a hundred years of Chinese Revolution.

References

1.   Mao, Zedong, *On Contradiction* (1937), *Marxist Internet Archive*, accessed 09 May 2021, <https://www.marxists.org/reference/archive/mao/selected-works/volume-1/mswv1_17.htm>

2.   Smedley, Agnes. *The Great Road: The Life and Times of Chu Teh*. United Kingdom: Monthly Review Press, 1972, p.vii

3.   Cited in Hinton, William. *Fanshen: A Documentary of Revolution in a Chinese Village*. New York: Monthly Review Press, 2008, p477

4.   Epstein, Israel. *From Opium War to Liberation*. Beijing: New World Press, 1956, p65

5.   *ibid*, p67

6.   Han, Suyin. *Eldest Son: Zhou Enlai and the Making of Modern China*. London: Pimlico, 1994, p39

7.   Alternatively romanised as *Kuomintang* (KMT)

8.   Lenin, V 1912, *Democracy and Narodism in China*, Marxist Internet Archive, accessed 09 May 2021, <https://www.marxists.org/archive/lenin/works/1912/jul/15.htm>.

9.   Hutchings, Graham. *China 1949: Year of Revolution*. London: Bloomsbury Academic, 2020, p17

10.   Snow, Edgar. *Red Star over China*. London: Grove Press UK, 2018, p98

11.   Mao, Z 1940, *On New Democracy*, Marxist Internet Archive, accessed 16 April 2021, .

12.   Hinton, *op cit*, p.xxiv

13.   Han, *op cit*, p178

14.   Snow, *op cit*, p185

15.   Cited in Snow, *ibid*, p276

16.   Hutchings, *op cit*, p44

17.   Mao, *On New Democracy*, *op cit*

18.   *ibid*

19.   Snow, *op cit*, p103

20.   Mao, Z 1940, *On the People's Democratic Dictatorship*, Marxist Internet Archive, accessed 22 April 2021, <https://www.marxists.org/reference/archive/mao/selected-works/volume-4/mswv4_65.htm>.

21.   Hutchings, *op cit*, p270

22.   Karl, Rebecca E.. *Mao Zedong and China in the Twentieth-Century World: A Concise History*. Ukraine: Duke University Press, 2010, p87

23.   Tsang, Steve Yui-Sang. *Cold War's Odd Couple: The Unintended Partnership between the Republic of China and the UK, 1950-1958*, 2021, p6

24.   Hutchings, *op cit*, p268

25.   *Statement Issued by the President, 27 June 1950*, The Office of the Historian, accessed 23 April 2021, <https://history.state.gov/historicaldocuments/frus1950v07/d119>.

26.   Mao, Z 1953, *Combat Bourgeois Ideas in the Party*, Marxist Internet Archive, accessed 23 April 2021, https://www.marxists.org/reference/archive/mao/selected-works/volume-5/mswv5_32.htm.

27.	Cited in Li, Mingjiang. *Mao's China and the Sino-Soviet Split: Ideological Dilemma*. Routledge Contemporary China Series 79. London ; New York: Routledge, 2012, p55.

28.	Karl, Rebecca E. *China's Revolutions in the Modern World: A Brief Interpretive History*. London ; New York: Verso, 2020, p129

29.	Prashad, Vijay. *The Poorer Nations: A Possible History of the Global South*. London ; New York: Verso, 2012, p199.

30.	Karl, *op cit*, p129

31.	Ji, Chaozhu. *The Man on Mao's Right: From Harvard Yard to Tiananmen Square, My Life inside China's Foreign Ministry*. New York: Random House, 2008, p195.

32.	Liu, Mingfu. *The China Dream: Great Power Thinking & Strategic Posture in the Post-American Era*. New York, NY: CN Times Books, 2015, p18.

33.	Han, *op cit*, p271

34.	Pantsov, Alexander, and Steven I. Levine. *Deng Xiaoping: A Revolutionary Life*. Oxford: Oxford University Press, 2015, p196

35.	Ji, *op cit*, p212

36.	Patnaik, U 2011, *Revisiting Alleged 30 Million Famine Deaths during China's Great Leap*, MR Online, accessed 24 April 2021, <https://mronline.org/2011/06/26/revisiting-alleged-30-million-famine-deaths-during-chinas-great-leap/>.

37.	Cited in Pantsov and Levine, *op cit*, p234

38.	*Circular of the Central Committee of the Communist Party of China on the Great Proletarian Cultural Revolution* (16 May 1966), Marxist Internet Archive, accessed 28 April 2021, <https://www.marxists.org/subject/china/documents/cpc/cc_gpcr.htm>.

39.	Mao, Z 1966, *A Letter To The Red Guards Of Tsinghua University Middle School*, Marxist Internet Archive, accessed 28 April 2021, <https://www.marxists.org/reference/archive/mao/selected-works/volume-9/mswv9_60.htm>.

40.	*Decision of the Central Committee of the Chinese Communist Party Concerning the Great Proletarian Cultural Revolution* (8 August 1966), Marxist Internet Archive, accessed 27 April 2021, <https://www.marxists.org/subject/china/peking-review/1966/PR1966-33g.htm>.

41.	Li, *op cit*, p134

42.	Han, *op cit*, p327

43.	Westad, Odd Arne. *The Global Cold War: Third World Interventions and the Making of Our Times*. 1st pbk. ed. Cambridge ; New York: Cambridge University Press, 2007, p163

44.	Han, *op cit*, p253

45.	Ji, *op cit*, p333

46.	Pantsov, Alexander, and Steven I. Levine. *Mao: The Real Story*. First Simon&Schuster paperback edition. New York: Simon & Schuster Paperbacks, 2013, p518

47.	Han, *op cit*, p387

48.	*Resolution on certain questions in the history of our party since the founding of the People's Republic of China (27 June 1981)*, Marxist Internet Archive, accessed 02 May 2021, <https://www.marxists.org/subject/china/documents/cpc/history/01.htm>.

49.	*ibid*

50.   Karl, *Mao Zedong and China in the Twentieth-Century World*, *op cit*, p119

51.   *Resolution on certain questions in the history of our party since the founding of the People's Republic of China (27 June 1981)*, *op cit*

52.   Ross, J 2019, *70 years of China's social miracle*, Socialist Economic Bulletin, accessed 02 May 2021, <https://www.socialisteconomicbulletin.net/2019/09/70-years-of-chinas-social-miracle/>.

53.   Deng, X 1978, *Emancipate the mind, seek truth from facts and unite as one in looking to the future*, China Daily, accessed 08 May 2021, <http://www.chinadaily.com.cn/china/19thcpcnationalcongress/2010-10/15/content_29714549.htm>.

54.   Deng, X 1984, *Building a Socialism with a Specifically Chinese Character*, China.org.cn, accessed 02 May 2021, <http://www.china.org.cn/english/features/dengxiaoping/103371.htm>.

55.   Sachs, Jeffrey. *The Ages of Globalization: Geography, Technology, and Institutions*. New York: Columbia University Press, 2020, p179

56.   Lin, Justin Yifu. *Demystifying the Chinese Economy*. Cambridge: Cambridge University Press, 2012, p6

57.   *ibid*, p153

58.   Cited in Pantsov and Levine, *Deng Xiaoping*, *op cit*, p337

59.   Deng, X 1982, *We shall concentrate on economic development*, People's Daily Online, accessed 04 May 2021, <http://en.people.cn/dengxp/vol3/text/c1030.html>.

60.   Saich, Tony., Yang, Benjamin. *The Rise to Power of the Chinese Communist Party: Documents and Analysis*. United States: Taylor & Francis, 2016.

61.   Marx, Karl. *Capital: A Critique of Political Economy. V. 3*: Penguin Classics. London ; New York, N.Y: Penguin Books in association with New Left Review, 1981, p368

62.   Deng, X 1985, *Reform is the only way for China to develop its productive forces*, China Daily, accessed 06 May 2021, <http://www.chinadaily.com.cn/china/19thcpcnationalcongress/2010-10/21/content_29714522.htm>.

63.   Xi, J 2013, *Uphold and Develop Socialism with Chinese Characteristics*, National People's Congress of the People's Republic of China, accessed 08 May 2021, <http://www.npc.gov.cn/englishnpc/c23934/202005/b04ff09d057b4c2d92fca94ca3fc8708.shtml>.

64.   Lenin, V 1921, *Report On The Substitution Of A Tax In Kind For The Surplus Grain Appropriation System*, Marxist Internet Archive, accessed 04 May 2021, <https://www.marxists.org/archive/lenin/works/1921/10thcong/ch03.htm>.

65.   Mao, Z 1957, *On the correct handling of contradictions among the people*, Marxist Internet Archive, accessed 07 May 2021, <https://www.marxists.org/reference/archive/mao/selected-works/volume-5/mswv5_58.htm>.

66.   Kroeber, Arthur R. *China's Economy: What Everyone Needs to Know*. New York, NY: Oxford University Press, 2016, p173

67.   Woodward, Jude. *The US vs China: Asia's New Cold War?* Geopolitical Economy. Manchester: Manchester University Press, 2017, p42

68.   Nolan, Peter. *Understanding China: The Silk Road and the Communist Manifesto*. Routledge Studies on the Chinese Economy 60. London ; New York: Routledge, Taylor & Francis Group, 2016, p2

69.   Deng, X 1987, *China can only take the socialist road*, China Daily, accessed 05 May 2021, <https://www.chinadaily.com.cn/china/19thcpcnationalcongress/2010-10/25/content_29714437.htm>.

70.   Mao, *On New Democracy, op cit*

71.   Deng, X 1985, *There is no fundamental contradiction between socialism and a market economy*, China Daily, accessed 10 May 2021, <http://www.chinadaily.com.cn/china/19thcpcnationalcongress/2010-10/21/content_29714520.htm>.

72.   Ross, John. *China's Great Road*. United States: People's Forum, 2021, p77

73.   Orlik, Thomas. *China: The Bubble That Never Pops*. Oxford: Oxford University Press, 2020, p149

74.   Han, *op cit*, p376

75.   *Memorandum by the President's Assistant for National Security Affairs (Kissinger) for the President's File. June 23, 1973*, Office of the Historian, accessed 07 May 2021, <https://history.state.gov/historicaldocuments/frus1969-76v15/d131>.

76.   Han, *op cit*, p251

77.   Zhou, E 1975, *Report on the Work of the Government*, Marxist Internet Archive, accessed 04 May 2021, <https://www.marxists.org/reference/archive/zhou-enlai/1975/01/13.htm>.

78.   Amin, Samir. *Beyond US Hegemony: Assessing the Prospects for a Multipolar World*. United Kingdom: Zed Books, 2013, p23

79.   Deng, X 1979, *Uphold the four cardinal principles*, China Daily, accessed 08 May 2021, <https://www.chinadaily.com.cn/china/19thcpcnationalcongress/2010-10/15/content_29714546.htm>.

80.   Hu, Angang. *China in 2020: A New Type of Superpower*. United States: Brookings Institution Press, 2012, p27

81.   Ross, *China's Great Road, op cit*, p19

82.   Xi, Jinping. *The Governance of China*. First edition. Beijing: Foreign Languages Press, 2014, p61

83.   Hutchings, *op cit*, p7

Will China Suffer the Same Fate as the Soviet Union?

Introduction

[1]We should think of China's communist regime quite differently from that of the USSR: it has, after all, succeeded where the Soviet Union failed. (Jacques 2009, 535)

This article addresses the reasons for the collapse of the Soviet Union, and seeks to understand whether the People's Republic of China (PRC) is vulnerable to the same forces that undermined the foundations of European socialism. What lessons can be drawn from the Soviet collapse? Has capitalism won? What future does socialism have in the world? Is there any escape for humanity from brutal exploitation, inequality and underdevelopment? Is there a future in which the world's billions can truly exercise their free will, their humanity, liberated from poverty and alienation?

The conclusions I draw are that China is following a fundamentally different path to that of the Soviet Union; that it has made a serious and comprehensive study of the Soviet collapse and rigorously applied what it has learnt; that the People's Republic of China remains a socialist country and the driving force towards a multipolar world; that, in spite of the rolling back of the first wave of socialist advance, Marxism remains as relevant as ever; and that, consequently, socialism has a bright future in the world.

---

[1] This article was first published in *World Review of Political Economy*, Vol. 11, No. 2 (Summer 2020): pp. 189-207.

Maintaining the Legitimacy of the CPC through Highly Effective Governance and Improvement in Living Standards

The Chinese experience since 1978 shows that a developing country must take the improvement of people's standard of living as its top priority. . . . With this belief, China has done its utmost to improve people's standard of living and achieved remarkable results in poverty eradication. (Zhang 2012, 96)

In the aftermath of the collapse of the Soviet Union and the European people's democracies between 1989 and 1991, many senior officials in China worried that the reform process could get out of hand. The Soviet leaders had attempted reform via *glasnost* and *perestroika*, and their experiments had ended in disaster. Wasn't this a cautionary message for the Communist Party of China (CPC) to return to the model of comprehensive state ownership and strictly centralised economic control?

Deng Xiaoping's insight was that the central element destabilising the Soviet Union wasn't its experiment with a mixed economy but its failure to deliver improvements in people's living standards. Economic stagnation from the mid-1970s onwards meant that people's basic expectations for a better life weren't being met. As a result, when it came to defending socialism from attack (both domestic and international), the masses couldn't easily be mobilised.

Deng understood that the Communist Party's legitimacy would only be maintained by eliminating poverty and improving people's everyday quality of life. Therefore, on his famous Southern Tour in 1992, he urged boldness rather than caution. As long as the CPC maintained political control, as long as the crucial parts of the economy (the "commanding heights") continued to be publicly owned, markets and foreign investment would benefit China. Attracted by the huge, well-educated and hardworking labour force, foreign companies would invest in China, thereby increasing China's capital and technical know-how, creating a virtuous cycle that would allow China to rise up the value chain and provide vastly improved living conditions to its population.

Decades later, it's uncontroversial to say that the economic strategy adopted in the period of "reform and opening up" (1978 onwards) has been highly successful. China's per capita income in 1979 was $210. Much of the rural population lived below the poverty line. Per capita food production had grown a total of just 10 percent from 1952. The PRC had fallen a long way behind the "East Asian miracle" zone (Japan, South Korea, China's Taiwan, China's Hong Kong, Singapore, Thailand, Malaysia and Indonesia) in terms of living standards. Justin Yifu Lin writes that the post-Mao leadership "had to improve national economic performance and make its people as rich as their neighbours, or it might lose support and its legitimacy for rule" (Lin 2012, 154).

In the following decades, the number of people in China living in "absolute poverty" (as defined by the World Bank) fell from 840 million to practically zero (Gupta 2020). Wages have increased continuously. Between 1988 and 2008, average per capita income grew by 229 percent, ten times the global average of 24 percent. In 1994, a Chinese factory worker made $500 a year, only a quarter of the wage of her counterpart in Thailand (Kroeber 2016, 174). In 2020, the average annual income in China exceeds $10,000—three times the figure for Thailand.

Although inequality has emerged as a serious problem, practically all Chinese people are substantially better off than they were 40 years ago in terms of nutrition, housing, clothing, access to services, and ability to travel. Consumer goods that were previously considered luxuries—such as washing machines, refrigerators, heated shower units, air conditioners, colour televisions, computers—can now be found in almost every home.

In the 2000s, the government re-established a comprehensive social security programme, including universal health insurance, free compulsory education for ages 6–15, pensions, subsidised housing, and income support. Workers' wages are increasing at a much faster rate than GDP, and as a result the income gap is starting to narrow.

Human Development Index (HDI) is a useful compound metric comprising life expectancy, educational level and per capita income. In HDI terms, China has risen from 0.407 in 1980 to 0.758 today (for calibration purposes, Norway is at the top of the charts with 0.949 and the Central African Republic at the bottom with 0.352). China's increase in HDI makes it the only country to leap-frog the "medium" HDI rank, moving from the "low HDI" group in 1990 to the "high HDI" group today (the requirement for the "very high HDI" group is 0.800—it's likely China will get there before the end of this decade).

Chinese productivity and innovation levels are gradually catching up with the most advanced capitalist countries, as the government's huge investment in science and technology reaps rewards. Veteran science writer Philip Ball notes that the patronising old idea that China . . . can imitate but not innovate is certainly false now. In several scientific fields, China is starting to set the pace for others to follow. On my tour of Chinese labs in 1992, only those I saw at the flagship Peking University looked comparable to what you might find at a good university in the West. Today the resources available to China's top scientists are enviable to many of their Western counterparts. (Ball 2018)

Whereas Soviet infrastructure was starting to crumble by the 1980s, modern Chinese infrastructure is world-class. Indeed, the quality of roads, trains, airports, ports and buildings in major Chinese cities is now noticeably higher than in global cities like New York and London.

The continuously improving economic situation and corresponding improvement in people's quality of life has led to strong popular support for the government and for Chinese socialism. The Pew Research Centre reports that President Xi Jinping enjoys a confidence rating of 94 percent,[1] which compares favourably with British Prime Minister Boris Johnson, whose approval rating is a mere 34 percent.[2] In 2014, 89 percent of Chinese rated their economy "good," compared with 64 percent for India and 40 percent for the US (Kroeber 2016, 198). British academic Peter Nolan writes that, "under Communist Party rule, China has experienced the most remarkable era of growth and development in modern history" (Nolan 2016, 2). Because of that, the rule of the Communist Party of China enjoys tremendous popular support and legitimacy.

Why Has Chinese Economic Reform Succeeded When the Soviet Reform Failed?

> *The vastly different results of the Russian and Chinese reforms are demonstrative of the critical importance of choosing the right reform strategies and paths. (Hu 2011, 28)*

The late Italian Marxist historian Domenico Losurdo noted that, in the 1930s and 40s, the Soviet "command economy" had worked extremely well: *"the rapid development of modern industry was interwoven with the construction of a welfare state that guaranteed the economic and social rights of citizens in a way that was unprecedented"* (Losurdo 2017, 17). However, after the period of frenetic building of socialism, followed by World War II, followed by reconstruction, came *"the transition from great historical crisis to a more 'normal' period"* [in which]*"the masses' enthusiasm and commitment to production and work weakened and then disappeared"* (Losurdo 2017, 17). In its final few years,

> [T]he Soviet Union was characterised by massive absenteeism and disengagement in the workplace: not only did production development stagnate, but there was no longer any application of the principle that Marx said drove socialism—remuneration according to the quantity and quality of work delivered. (Losurdo 2017, 17)

From the mid-1970s onwards, the Soviet economy entered a period of slow economic growth, just at the point when the major capitalist countries were starting to leverage developments in technology and management to achieve major steps forward in productivity. Jude Woodward notes that,

> from 20 per cent of the size of the US economy in 1944, the Soviet economy peaked at 44 per cent that of the US by 1970 ($1,352 billion to $3,082 billion) but had fallen back to 36 per cent of the US by 1989 ($2,037 billion to $5,704 billion). It never came near challenging the economic weight of the US. (Woodward 2017, chapter 16, 248)

Losurdo contends that China in the late 1970s faced very similar problems:

> The China that arose from the Cultural Revolution resembled the Soviet Union to an extraordinary degree in its last years of existence: the socialist principle of compensation based on the amount and quality of work delivered was substantially liquidated, and disaffection, disengagement, absenteeism and anarchy reigned in the workplace. (Losurdo 2017, 19)

China had made remarkable progress in terms of life expectancy, land ownership, social equality, education and mass empowerment since the birth of the People's Republic in 1949, yet by the late 1970s it was still a long way from being an advanced country. Hundreds of millions of people in the villages faced food insecurity and poor housing conditions.

Being a poor country with a tremendous responsibility to meet the immediate needs of its huge population, China lacked the resources to invest heavily in research and development, and the resulting low productivity meant that it couldn't guarantee an adequate standard of living to its people. Cut off from the global marketplace, it wasn't able to quickly learn from others or benefit from an ever-more globalised division of labour. There was a shortage of capital, a low level of technological development, and a lack of incentives for production and innovation. Much as with the Soviet Union in its later decades, China's planning system continued to be overly reliant on voluntarism and "moral incentives" to raise production. The history of socialist economics over the last century indicates that such an approach suffers from diminishing returns and can't be sustained forever.

This is the context in which reform and opening up was adopted in the late 1970s. Superficially, the reform strategy pursued by China from 1978 shares some similarity with the various attempts at economic reform in the Soviet Union, particularly the set of policies introduced by the Gorbachev leadership under the umbrella of *perestroika*. However, there are profound differences between the Chinese and Soviet approaches that help to explain the unquestionable success of one and the comprehensive failure of the other.

China's approach to reform was extremely cautious and pragmatic, *"based on a step-by-step, piecemeal and experimental approach. If a reform worked it was extended to new areas; if it failed then it was abandoned" (Jacque 2009, 176)*. All reforms had to be tested in practice, all results had to be analysed, and all analysis had to inform future experiments. Chen Yun, the lead economist of the Deng era, stated in 1980 that

> the steps must be steady, because we shall encounter many complicated problems. So do not rush. . . . We should proceed with experiments, review our experience from time to time, and correct mistakes whenever

we discover them, so that minor mistakes will not grow into major ones. (Hu 2011, 33)

Many key reform concepts came from the grass-roots. *"We processed their ideas and raised them to the level of guidelines for the whole country. Practice is the sole criterion for testing truth"* *(Deng 1992).*

Reform in China was patient, incremental and results-oriented, whereas *"Gorbachev made the fatal mistake of trying to do too much, too fast"* (Shambaugh 2008, 65). Gorbachev's reforms were implemented in a heavy-handed, top-down way, without leveraging the ideas and creativity of the masses or attempting to collate feedback. Given that the project was presented as a form of "democratisation," it's ironic that it was carried out in a profoundly undemocratic manner. The leadership didn't mobilise the existing, proven structures of society (the soviets and the Communist Party) but sought to bypass and weaken them.

Instead of relying on the most pragmatic elements of the party and state officialdom in restructuring of the country, Gorbachev tried to build up new political forces and movements while gradually diminishing the power of the party and of centralised state structures (Zubok 2007, 307).

The media wasn't used to unite the people behind a programme of development but to denigrate the Communist Party. The economic programme was incoherent and subject to sudden changes in direction. The result was, in the words of veteran Russian communist Gennady Zyuganov, *"a parade of political arrogance, demagoguery, and dilettantism, which gradually overwhelmed and paralysed the country"* *(Zyuganov 1997, 107).*

The Chinese and Soviet economies in the 1970s both suffered from a stifling over-centralisation. China's reform process addressed this imbalance in a gradual manner, in which *"the relaxation of restrictions on private capital development was combined with state control and planned and state-led heavy investment" (Roberts 2017).* In the Soviet Union, by contrast, the planning agencies were simply dismantled overnight, creating chaos throughout the economy.

Although China's reform process served to introduce market forces into the economy, the whole process was carried out under the tight control of the government and took place within the context of a planned economy. The level of marketisation that has taken place in China is far greater than that which took place in the Soviet Union; however, China also maintained stronger macroeconomic control. Even now, after more than four decades of economic reform, "the state remains firmly in command" of the Chinese economy. "The government will pursue reforms that increase the role of the market in setting prices, but will avoid reforms that permit the market to transfer control of assets from the state to the private sector" (Kroeber 2016, 225).

Peter Nolan, no means a cheerleader for centrally-planned economies, writes: *"The comparison of the experience of China and Russia's reforms confirms that, at certain junctures and in certain countries, effective planning is a necessary condition of economic success" (Nolan 1995, 312).* Nolan (1995, 160–175) points out that the Chinese state took the lead in conducting large-scale experiments and analysing the results; protecting domestic industry from the sudden appearance of foreign goods; supporting the growth of the state-owned enterprises to a level where they could become competitive in the global marketplace; investing in social and economic infra-structure (transport, healthcare, education, power generation); and coordinating the different parts of the reform programme.

David Kotz and Fred Weir observe that there was hardly any privatisation in the Chinese reform process—state enterprises were kept under state ownership and control.

> There was no sudden price liberalisation—state enter-prises continued to sell at controlled prices. Central planning was retained for the state sector of the econ-omy. Rather than slashing state spending, various lev-els of government poured funds into improving China's basic economic infrastructure of transportation, com-munication, and power. Rather than tight monetary pol-icy, ample credit was provided for expansion and mod-ernisation. The state has sought to gradually develop a market economy over a period of decades, and the state has actively guided the process. (*Kotz and Weir 1997, 197*)

The result was a far more effective programme of eco-nomic reform than that which took place in the Soviet Union from 1985–1991 or in post-Soviet Russia from 1991 onwards.

If "the proof of the pudding is in the eating," then Chi-nese dessert has proven itself to be far tastier than its Soviet counterpart. *Perestroika* turned a sluggish economy into a fail-ing one. By 1991, the last year of the USSR's existence, the economy was contracting at a rate of 15 percent per year. Gor-bachev's blind faith in the inherent corrective power of the mar-ket turned out to be misplaced; investment collapsed. "Net fixed investment declined at the astounding rate of 21 per cent in 1990 and an estimated 25 per cent in 1991" (Kotz and Weir 1997, 97).

In China, GDP growth increased from around 4 percent in the 1970s to nearly 10 percent in the period from 1978 to 1992. Since 1978, China's economy has grown more than any other country; it also tops the list for growth of per capita GDP, which has risen from $156 in 1978 to just over $10,000 at the time of writing.

China Is Not Weakening Communist Party Rule or Attacking Its Own History

If China allowed bourgeois liberalisation, there would inevitably be turmoil. We would accomplish nothing, and our principles, policies, line and development strategy would all be doomed to failure. (Deng 2007)

In both China and the Soviet Union, market-oriented economic reform meant breaking with past policy to some degree. A major difference is that in the Soviet Union, this change of policy was accompanied by a concerted attempt to undermine the legitimacy of the Communist Party and the confidence of the people in their history.

In 1986, Gorbachev and his advisers came up with the concept of *glasnost*—"openness"—to encapsulate policies of greater government transparency, wider political discussion and increased popular participation. The idea seemed unobjectionable to begin with, but glasnost soon became a battle cry for an all-out attack on the legitimacy of Communist Party rule and a powerful weapon in the hands of class forces hostile to socialism.

Faced with significant opposition to their economic proposals within the Communist Party, and lacking a base among the masses, Gorbachev's team increasingly looked to "liberal reformers" for support—people who supported perestroika and wanted it to be accompanied by a transition towards a European-style parliamentary political system. These reformers encouraged Gorbachev to engineer a quiet coup in the name of democracy, ending the Communist Party's leading role in the government by dismantling the Supreme Soviet and replacing it with a Congress of People's Deputies. Representatives to this latter body were directly elected, but the selection of candidates was heavily manipulated in favour of pro-perestroika, pro-Western Gorbachev loyalists.

Cheng and Liu observe that,

> in the name of promoting young cadres and of reform, Gorbachev replaced large numbers of party, political and military leaders with anti-CPSU and anti-socialist cadres or cadres with ambivalent positions. This practice laid the foundations, in organisational and cadre selection terms, for the political "shift of direction." (Cheng and Liu 2017, 305)

Yegor Ligachev, a high-ranking Soviet official who observed all this firsthand, supports this conclusion.

> *What happened in our country is primarily the result of the debilitation and eventual elimination of the Communist Party's leading role in society, the ejection of the party from major policymaking, its ideological and organisational unravelling (Ligachev 1996, 286).*

The political transformation was supported by a thoroughgoing media campaign denigrating Soviet history, vastly exaggerating the excesses and mistakes of the Stalin period, and even attacking the Soviet Union's role in the Second World War. Things went so far that Cuban leader Fidel Castro was prompted to comment in 1989:

> *It's impossible to carry out a revolution or conduct a rectification without a strong, disciplined and respected party. It's not possible to carry out such a process by slandering socialism, destroying its values, discrediting the party, demoralising its vanguard, abandoning its leadership role, eliminating social discipline, and sowing chaos and anarchy everywhere. This may foster a counter-revolution—but not revolutionary change. . . . It is disgusting to see how many people, even in the Soviet Union itself, are engaged in denying and destroying the history-making feats and extraordinary merits of that heroic people. (Castro 2013, 56)*

The Communist Party had been the major vehicle for promoting the needs and ideas of the Soviet working class; once it was sidelined, the workers had no obvious means of organising in defence of their interests. This opened up a space for a pro-capitalist minority to dominate political power and, ultimately, break up the country and dismantle socialism.

The Chinese leadership understood that the People's Republic of China could not survive without the continued leadership of the Communist Party, and this is a key lesson that it has learned from the collapse of the Soviet Union. Xi Jinping notes that

> [O]ne important reason for the disintegration of the Soviet Union and the collapse of the CPSU is the complete denial of the history of the Soviet Union, and the history of the CPSU, the denial of Lenin and other leading

personalities, and historical nihilism confused the people's thoughts. (cited in Rudolph and Szonyi 2018, 23)

There was no appetite whatsoever for transplanting the political ideas of the American and European bourgeoisie onto Chinese soil. According to Weiwei Zhang, who worked as an interpreter for Deng Xiaoping, Deng was completely focused on the main task: improving people's livelihoods. Any political reform should be conducted not for its own sake but only to the extent that it served the overall goal.

> He believed that copying the Western model and placing political reform on the top of the agenda, like the Soviets were doing at the time, was utterly foolish. In fact, that was exactly Deng's comment on Gorbachev after their meeting: 'This man may look smart but in fact is stupid. (Zhang 2014)

In a changing economic environment, where private capital was being accumulated and a new class of entrepreneurs emerging, continued Communist Party rule was essential to guarantee that development benefitted the masses and that the new owners of capital didn't become politically dominant. Moreover, political stability was an absolute requirement for successful economic reform.

In practically every important speech on China's development path from 1978 until his death in 1997, Deng insisted on what he termed the Four Cardinal Principles: 1) Defend the socialist path; 2) Maintain the dictatorship of the proletariat (working class rule); 3) Maintain the leadership of the party; and 4) Adhere to Marxism-Leninism and Mao Zedong Thought. He was extremely clear regarding the importance of a workers' state:

What kind of democracy do the Chinese people need today? It can only be socialist democracy, people's democracy, and not bourgeois democracy. . . . Personal interests must be subordinated to collective ones, the interests of the part to those of the whole, and immediate to long-term interests. In other words, limited interests must be subordinated to overall interests, and minor interests to major ones. . . . It is still necessary to exercise dictatorship over all these anti-socialist elements. . . . The fact of the matter is that socialism cannot be defended or built up without the dictatorship of the proletariat. (Deng 2001, 183)

The CPC has not followed the Soviet example of attacking its own history. Although the Chinese leadership made serious criticisms of certain policies associated with Mao (in particular the Great Leap Forward and the Cultural Revolution), it has never come anywhere close to repudiating Mao and undermining the basic ideological and historical foundations of Chinese socialism. No Chinese Wall has been constructed between the Mao-era and the post-Mao era; the two phases are inextricably linked, and are both "pragmatic explorations in building socialism conducted by the people under the leadership of the Party" (Xi 2014, 47).

We will forever keep Chairman Mao's portrait on Tiananmen Gate as a symbol of our country, and we will always remember him as a founder of our Party and state. . . . We will not do to Chairman Mao what Khrushchev did to Stalin. (Deng 1980)

The CPSU leadership suffered a crisis of legitimacy that it had created. Gorbachev and his colleagues attacked and weakened the organs of working-class rule. They colluded in the transfer of political power to anti-socialist forces. Meanwhile in China, "the rule of the Communist Party is no longer in doubt: it enjoys the prestige that one would expect given the transformation that it has presided over" (Jacques 2009, 277).

In addition to its successes in the economic realm, the CPC has also led a process of unification, stabilisation and recovery following the "century of humiliation," which started with the First Opium War (1839–1842) and ended with the founding of the People's Republic of China in 1949. The Chinese political system has been extraordinarily effective in protecting China's independence and national integrity, and this is the pre-eminent factor in the Chinese people's support for the CPC-led government.

China Has Managed to Avoid a Superpower "Cold War"

The last thing China wants is war. China is very poor and wants to develop; it can't do that without a peaceful environment. Since we want a peaceful environment, we must cooperate with all of the world's forces for peace. (Deng 1984)

The necessity of maintaining peaceful relations with the imperialist world has been a preoccupation of socialist states from 1917 onwards. All socialist leaderships—those of Lenin, Stalin, Mao, Ho Chi Minh, Kim Il Sung and Fidel Castro included—have pursued "peaceful coexistence" to the extent that it has been possible.

The importance of international peace for China's development was implicitly recognised by Mao in the early 1970s, when Henry Kissinger's visit to Beijing opened the way for the PRC finally taking its seat at the UN. Continuing US-China communications throughout the 1970s led to the establishment of formal diplomatic relations between China and the US in 1979. Ever since, China has managed to maintain peaceful and mutually beneficial relations with the capitalist world.

Peaceful coexistence has required compromises, one of which has been China relinquishing a direct leadership role in the global transition to socialism. The Soviet Union took on a heavy responsibility as the global centre of anti-imperialist forces, giving extensive practical solidarity to socialist states, national liberation movements and progressive governments around the world—including vast economic support to the People's Republic of China between 1949 and 1959; military and economic support to Cuba, Vietnam, Afghanistan, Angola, Nicaragua, Korea, Ethiopia and elsewhere; training, aid and weapons to the ANC (African National Congress) in South Africa, Frelimo in Mozambique, Swapo in South West Africa (now Namibia), PAIGC (Partido Africano da Independência da Guiné e Cabo Verde) in Guinea Bissau, and others.

In addition to direct aid, the Soviet role as the protector of the progressive world—and its position as one of two "superpowers"—meant that it was forced to devote an extraordinary portion of its resources to military development. The figures vary wildly, but Russian-American historian Alexander Pantsov estimates that, *"at the start of Gorbachev's perestroika, in 1985, the Soviets were spending 40 percent of their budget on defence."* Indeed, Pantsov concludes that *"the economy of the USSR collapsed under the burden of military expenditures"* (Pantsov and Levine 2015, 432). US President Ronald Reagan developed a "full-court press" strategy in the early 1980s that sought to vastly increase US military expenditure, forcing the USSR to follow suit and thereby deepen its economic difficulties.

The Soviet Union had long stuck to a system of "strategic parity" of nuclear weapons development, sparing no effort to keep up with (but not surpass) the US. As long as it had the ability to retaliate against any US-initiated nuclear strike, it could basically guarantee that such a strike wouldn't take place. However, the economic burden of it was enormous. In a capitalist society, the arms industry is a highly profitable field of investment; creating demand for weapons is a boon for private capital. In a socialist society with a strong responsibility towards catering to the basic needs of its population, arms manufacturing means diverting human and material resources away from those basic needs.

This was not a situation of the Soviet Union's making, but one that was forced on it by a US-led Western imperialist strategy that was hell-bent on undermining European socialism. Indeed, the Soviet leaders routinely proposed multilateral disarmament and a thawing of the Cold War. Boris Ponomarev, Chief of the International Department of the CPSU Central Committee from 1955 to 1986, wrote:

> The US has taken the initiative all along in developing and perfecting nuclear weapons and their delivery vehicles ever since the advent of the atom bomb. Each time the USSR was forced to respond to the challenge to strengthen its own defences, to protect the countries of the socialist community and to keep its armed forces adequately equipped with up-to-date weaponry. But the Soviet Union has been and remains the most consistent advocate of the limitation of the arms race, a champion

of disarmament under effective international control. (Ponomarev 1983, 53)

Furthermore, by the late 1970s, the Cold War had turned decidedly hot. The Western powers were engaged in a massive "rollback" operation, supporting rebellions against progressive governments in Angola, Afghanistan, Nicaragua, Ethiopia, Mozambique, Cambodia and South Yemen. Vijay Prashad writes that the CIA and the Pentagon *"abandoned the idea of the mere 'containment' of communism in favour of using military force to push back against its exertions" (Prashad 2012, 112)*. All the states under attack had an urgent need for military and civilian aid, which the Soviet Union had little choice but to provide.

The peak of this "hot" Cold War was in Afghanistan, where the leftist People's Democratic Party of Afghanistan (PDPA) government pleaded with the Soviet leaders to help them quell an Islamic fundamentalist rebellion that was generously funded and armed by the US.

The first Russian troops crossed the border into Afghanistan on December 25, 1979. The scope of their mission was limited: try to restore unity within the PDPA, help the Afghan Army gain the upper hand against the uprising, and come home soon.

> The aim was not to take over or occupy the country. It was to secure the towns and the roads between them, and to withdraw as soon as the Afghan government and its armed forces were in a state to take over the responsibility for themselves. (Braithwaite 2012, 123)

The intervention turned out to be much more difficult, complex and prolonged than the Soviets had imagined. Their

Afghan allies were divided and often demoralised; meanwhile their enemies were armed with sophisticated weaponry, had significant support among the rural population, were fuelled by a vehement hatred of the Russians, and were able to leverage Afghanistan's mountainous territory to their advantage. Meanwhile the Red Army was not trained for a counter-insurgency war. The last major war it had fought was World War II. Odd Arne Westad writes that

> *from 1981 onwards the war turned into a bloody stalemate, in which more than one million Afghans died and at least 25,000 Soviets. In spite of well-planned efforts, the Red Army simply could not control the areas that were within their operational zones—they advanced into rebel strongholds, kept them occupied for weeks or months, and then had to withdraw as the Mujahedin concentrated its forces or, more often, because its opponents attacked elsewhere. (Westad 2007, 356)*

The Red Army didn't lose any of its major battles in Afghanistan; it won control of hundreds of towns, villages and roads, only to lose them again when its focus moved elsewhere. The US deployed increasingly sophisticated weaponry to the rebel groups at just the right rate so as to prolong the war.

The Red Army began a phased withdrawal on May 15, 1988. It had not been defeated as such, but it had manifestly failed in its objectives of cementing PDPA rule and suppressing the rebellion. Meanwhile, the Soviet Union had expended vast economic, military and human resources. Thousands of young lives were lost. Soviet diplomatic clout had been reduced. The CPSU's popular legitimacy was damaged, just as had been hoped by US strategists—Zbigniew Brzezinski, who was US National Security Advisor at the time of the Soviet intervention,

and who had talked specifically about "the opportunity of giving to the USSR its Vietnam war" (Brzezinski 1998).
Afghanistan and the arms race were by no means the sole—or even primary—factor in the Soviet Union's demise, but they certainly contributed.

China on the other hand has been able to enjoy a long period of peace. The Chinese People's Volunteer Army proved during the Korean War (the War to Resist US Agression and Aid Korea) of 1950–1953 that People's China was willing and able to defend itself from attack, and no doubt the US drew the appropriate lesson that any military operation against it would be highly risky.

The post-1978 leadership of the CPC realised that, by inserting China into the emerging global supply chains, China could become sufficiently important to the functioning of the global economy that the imperialist states would have to think very carefully about the wisdom of attacking or isolating it. Jude Woodward notes that China's rise has forced many countries to pursue good relations with it, even if they oppose its ideology.

> Rather developed neighbours such as South Korea or [China's] Taiwan are deeply economically engaged with [the mainland of] China and do not want this derailed. . . . Even America's European allies, notably Germany, France and Britain, were prepared to ignore US opinion on China when they signed up to the AIIB [Asian Infrastructure Investment Bank]. (Woodward 2017, chapter 16, 251)

This could be thought of as a sort of strategic parity with Chinese characteristics, with a much lower price tag than its Soviet equivalent. Additionally, China's integration in the world economy has allowed it to be a part of *"the unprece-dented global technological revolution, offering a short cut for the country to accelerate its industrial transformation and up-grade its economic structure"* *(Clegg 2009, chapter 7, 129).*

In the relatively safe international environment con-structed by the PRC government, China has been able to reduce its military spending from around 7 percent of GDP in 1978 to around 2 percent currently, allowing more resources to be de-voted to improving living standards. Although its strategy doesn't allow it to play an active military role in the defence of friendly states and movements, China's economic strength means that it is able to provide crucial support for progressive countries around the world.

Conclusion

So long as socialism does not collapse in China, it will always hold its ground in the world. (Deng 2007)

It was widely assumed in the West following the col-lapse of European socialism that China would undergo a similar process of counter-revolution. Three decades on, it's abun-dantly clear that China is not following the same trajectory. Its reform process has been highly successful; the quality of life of its people continues to improve; it is emerging as a global leader in science, technological innovation and environmental preser-vation; nationalist separatism is being effectively contained; and the Communist Party of China remains popular and hege-monic. In short, China has continued to develop a form of so-cialism that is appropriate to its own conditions.

This does not of course imply that the People's Repub-lic of China doesn't face serious problems. Rapid development has engendered unprecedented levels of inequality and environmental destruction. While standard of living has increased at all levels of the population, income inequality is stark, and this is a source of considerable social friction. Meanwhile the policy of focusing development on the Eastern and Southern coastal cities has led to regional disparities. The CPC government has been particularly focused on these problems over the last 10–15 years, for example, narrowing regional inequality via preferential investment in poorer areas. Meanwhile China has taken significant strides in improving its environmental record, emerging as a leading force in the global battle against climate breakdown (Finamore 2018).

Chinese economists often talk of the "latecomers' advantage" in the world of technology, whereby *"technological innovation and industrial upgrading can be achieved by imitation, import, and/or integration of existing technologies and industries, all of which implies much lower R&D costs" (Lin 2013).* There's a sense in which this idea applies to the world of politics as well. The USSR was the world's first socialist state, and as such its successes and mistakes constitute indispensable raw material for the study of socialist society. The CPC has been assiduous in learning from the Soviet demise in order to avoid suffering a similar fate. David Shambaugh, citing a study by the Chinese Academy of Social Sciences, sums up some of the key lessons the CPC has tried to absorb. These include

> concentrating on economic development and continuously improving people's standard of living," "upholding Marxism as the guiding ideology," "strengthening party leadership," and "continuously strengthening efforts on party building—especially in the areas of ideology, image, organisation, and democratic centralism—in order to safeguard the leadership power in the

hands of loyal Marxists. (Shambaugh 2008, 77; emphasis in the original)

The issue of maintaining a workers' state and preventing the ascendance and dominance of pro-capitalist "liberals" is arguably the most important lesson to be learned from the collapse of the USSR. Even with ongoing economic difficulties, it's perfectly conceivable that Soviet socialism could have survived if the top leadership hadn't effectively abandoned the project. In that sense, Gorbachev and his close collaborators bear significant responsibility for the Soviet demise. Allen Lynch, a researcher of Russian politics at the University of Virginia, speculates that, if Gorbachev's predecessor Yuri Andropov had lived longer (he died at the age of 69 after just one year as General Secretary of the CPSU), things might have been very different.

> Judging from Andropov's programmatic statements in 1982–83, as well as his long record at the summit of Soviet politics, there can be little doubt that he would not have countenanced anything remotely resembling Gorbachev's political reforms or that he would have hesitated to use force to stop public challenges to communist rule. Moreover, Andropov's networks in the Party, KGB, government and military were incomparably stronger than Gorbachev's and he might well have leveraged a viable coalition for piecemeal reform of the Soviet economy. (Lynch 2012)

Therefore, the dissolution of Soviet Union is not caused by socialist institution or system itself. Instead, it is an inevitable result of the betray of Gorbachev and Yeltin's leadership to socialism. The lessons from the collapse of the Soviet Union must be thoroughly learned by the remaining—and future—socialist states as well as the global working class as a whole. In the current stage of history, where these states constitute a minority and where they face a powerful ideological enemy that is determined to undermine them, these lessons are broadly applicable. They form a key part of the great legacy that the Soviet experience leaves to the global working class.

The Soviet project is by no means a historical relic; its experience is relevant and even crucial to contemporary politics. The heroic feats of the Soviet people live on in China, Vietnam, Cuba, Laos and Korea; in socialist-oriented and progressive states and movements around the world. Even in the territories of the former Soviet Union and the former socialist states in Europe, the memory of better times lives on (not least in the considerable defence and retention of Soviet achievements, traditions and forms in Belarus). Their populations are starting, as Fidel Castro predicted they would, to regret the counter-revolution, to miss *those orderly countries, where everyone had clothes, food, medicine, education, and there was no crime, no mafia*"; they are beginning to *"realise the great historic mistake they made when they destroyed socialism" (Castro 1995)*.

The socialist project lives on in China and becomes stronger every day. As quality of life gradually catches up with and outstrips that in the leading capitalist countries, and as China emerges as a global leader in science and technology and as a force for peace, multipolarity and environmental preservation, Chinese socialism will become widely recognised as a highly effective, creative and adaptive branch of Marxism.

Notes

1. See "Confidence in the Chinese President," Pew Research Centre Global Indicators Database, Spring 2019. Accessed April 28, 2020.
https://www.pewresearch.org/global/database/indicator/69/country/cn/.

2. See "Yougov Public Figure: Boris Johnson," February 2020, accessed April 28, 2020,
https://yougov.co.uk/topics/politics/explore/public_figure/Boris_Johnson.

References

Ball, P. 2018. "China's Great Leap Forward in Science." *The Guardian*, February18. Accessed April 28, 2020. https://www.theguardian.com/science/2018/feb/18/china-great-leap-forward-science-research-innovation-investment-5g-genetics-quantum-internet.

Braithwaite, R. 2012. *Afgantsy: The Russians in Afghanistan 1979–89*. London: Profile Books.

Brzezinski, Z. 1998. "Interview with Le Nouvel Observateur." Accessed April 28, 2020. https://dgibbs.faculty.arizona.edu/brzezinski_interview.

Castro, F. 1995. "Discurso pronunciado por Fidel Castro Ruz, Presidente de la República de Cuba, en la recepción efectuada en el Palacio de la Reunificacion. Ciudad Ho Chi Minh, Viet Nam, 10 de diciembre de 1995" [Address by Fidel Castro Luz, President of the Republic of Cuba, at a Reception at the Palace of Unification. Ho Chi Minh City, Vietnam, 10 December 1995]. *Cuba.cu.* Accessed February 18, 2021. http://www.cuba.cu/gobierno/discursos/1995/esp/f101295e.html.

Castro, F. 2013. *Cuba and Angola: Fighting for Africa's Freedom and Our Own*. New York, NY: Pathfinder Press.

Cheng, E., and Z. Liu. 2017. "The Historical Contribution of the October Revolution to the Economic and Social Development of the Soviet Union—Analysis of the Soviet

Economic Model and the Causes of Its Dramatic End." *International Critical Thought* 7 (3): 297–308.

Clegg, J. 2009.*China's Global Strategy: Towards a Multipolar World.* London: Pluto Press.

Deng, X. 1980. "Answers to the Italian Journalist Oriana Fallaci." *People.cn*, August 21. Accessed April 28, 2020. http://en.people.cn/dengxp/vol2/text/b1470.html.

Deng, X. 1984. "We Regard Reform as a Revolution." *China.org.cn*, October10. Accessed April 28, 2020. http://www.china.org.cn/english/features/dengxiaoping/103366.htm.

Deng, X. 1992. "Excerpts from Talks Given in Wuchang, Shenzhen, Zhuhai and Shanghai." *People.cn*. Accessed April 28, 2020. http://en.people.cn/dengxp/vol3/text/d1200.html.

Deng, X. 2001. "Uphold the Four Cardinal Principles (1979)." In *Selected Works of Deng Xiaoping, 1975–1982*, 166–191. Honolulu, HI: University Press of the Pacific.

Deng, X. 2007. "We Must Adhere to Socialism: A Talk with Julius Kambarage Nyerere, Former President of Tanzania, Chairman of the Tanzanian Revolutionary Party and Chairman of the South Commission, November 23, 1989." *China Daily*. Accessed April 28, 2020. http://www.chinadaily.com.cn/china/2007-09/30/content_6148311.htm.

Finamore, B. 2018. *Will China Save the Planet? Environmental Futures*. Cambridge: Polity Books.

Gupta, R. 2020. "China on Target to Eliminate Extreme Poverty by 2020." *China.org.cn*, January 21. Accessed April 28, 2020. http://www.china.org.cn/opinion/2020-01/21/content_75636612.htm.

Hu, A. 2011. *China in 2020: A New Type of Superpower*. Washington, DC: Brookings Institution Press.

Jacques, M. 2009. *When China Rules the World: The End of the Western World and the Birth of a New Global Order.* New York: Penguin Press.

Kotz, D. M., and F. Weir. 1997. *Revolution from Above: The Demise of the Soviet System*. New York: Routledge.

Kroeber, A. R. 2016. *China's Economy: What Everyone Needs to Know*. New York: Oxford University Press.

Ligachev, Y. 1996. *Inside Gorbachev's Kremlin: The Memoirs of Yegor*. Boulder, CO: Westview Press.

Lin, J. Y. 2012. *Demystifying the Chinese Economy*. Cambridge: Cambridge University Press.

Lin, J. Y. 2013. "Advantage of Being a Latecomer." *China.org.cn*, August 7. Accessed April 28, 2020. http://www.china.org.cn/opinion/2013-08/07/content_29646629.htm.

Losurdo, D. 2017. "Has China Turned to Capitalism? Reflections on the Transition from Capitalism to Socialism." *International Critical Thought* 7 (1) 2017: 15–31.

Lynch, A. 2012. "Deng's and Gorbachev's Reform Strategies Compared." *Russia in Global Affairs*, June 24. Accessed April 28, 2020. https://eng.globalaffairs.ru/articles/dengs-and-gorbachevs-reform-strategies-compared/.

Nolan, P. 1995.*China's Rise, Russia's Fall: Politics, Economics and Planning in the Transition from Stalinism*. New York: St. Martin's Press.

Nolan, P. 2016. *Understanding China: The Silk Road and the Communist Manifesto*. New York: Routledge.

Pantsov, A, and S. Levine. 2015. *Deng Xiaoping: A Revolutionary Life*. Oxford: Oxford University Press.

Ponomarev, B. N. 1983. *Marxism-Leninism in Today's World, a Living and Effective Teaching: A Reply to Critics*. 1st English ed. Oxford: Pergamon Press.

Prashad, V. 2012. *The Poorer Nations: A Possible History of the Global South*. London: Verso.

Roberts, M. 2017. "The Russian Revolution: Some Economic Notes." Michael Robert's Blog, November 8. Accessed April 28, 2020. https://thenextrecession.wordpress.com/2017/11/08/the-russian-revolution-some-economic-notes/.

Rudolph, J. M., and M. Szonyi, eds. 2018.*The China Questions: Critical Insights into a Rising Power*. Cambridge, MA: Harvard University Press.

Shambaugh, D. L. 2008. *China's Communist Party: Atrophy and Adaptation*. Washington, DC: Woodrow Wilson Center Press.

Westad, O. A. 2007. *The Global Cold War: Third World Interventions and the Making of Our Times*. Cambridge: Cambridge University Press.

Woodward, J. 2017. *The US vs China: Asia's New Cold War?* Manchester: Manchester University Press.

Xi, J. 2014. *Xi Jinping: The Governance of China*, vol. 1. Beijing: Foreign Languages Press.

Zhang, W. 2012. *The China Wave: Rise of a Civilizational State*. Hackensack, NJ: World Century.

Zhang, W. 2014. "My Personal Memories as Deng Xiaoping's Interpreter: From Oriana Fallaci to Kim Il-sung to Gorbachev." *Guancha*, August 26. Accessed April 28, 2020. https://www.guancha.cn/ZhangWeiWei/2014_08_26_260544.shtml.

Zubok, V. M. 2007. *A Failed Empire: The Soviet Union in the Cold War from Stalin to Gorbachev—The New Cold War History*. Chapel Hill: University of North Carolina Press.

Zyuganov, G. 1997. *Gennady My Russia: The Political Autobiography of Gennady Zyuganov Armonk*. New York: M. E. Sharpe.

The CPC: The Most Successful Political Party in History

[2]The 20th National Congress of the Communist Party of China (CPC), which commenced on October 16, 2022, is seen as a milestone event in the history of the CPC.

In the Report delivered by Xi Jinping, general secretary of the CPC Central Committee, to the Congress, major achievements that the country has accomplished over the past 10 years were summarized.

A decade ago, Xi Jinping put forward the Two Centenary goals: to achieve a "moderately prosperous society in all respects" by the centenary of the CPC in 2021, and a "great modern socialist country that is prosperous, strong, democratic, culturally advanced, harmonious and beautiful" by the centenary of the founding of the People's Republic of China in 2049.

The core component of achieving a "moderately prosperous society in all respects" was the campaign to alleviate extreme poverty. This goal was achieved in late 2020 – remarkably, whilst China was concurrently battling the COVID-19 pandemic (a pandemic which has sadly resulted in a dramatic rise in poverty in many countries around the world). At the start of the targeted poverty alleviation program in 2014, just under 100 million people were identified as living below the poverty line; seven years later, the number was zero.

United Nations Secretary-General Antonio Guterres stated that China had carried out "the greatest anti-poverty

---

[2] This article was first published in *China Today* (October 19, 2022): http://www.chinatoday.com.cn/cteng-lish/2018/hotspots/2022spdh/china_in_for-eign_eyes/202210/t20221019_800310760.html

achievement in history." To eradicate extreme poverty in a developing country of 1.4 billion people – which at the time of the founding of the People's Republic of China in 1949 was one of the poorest countries in the world – is without a doubt an extraordinary accomplishment.

Why China? Why is it China and not another country that has carried out the most comprehensive poverty elimination in history? How has China been able to leap from a state of intense poverty, underdevelopment and backwardness just 73 years ago to becoming a country with the second-largest economy in the world, with the average life expectancy of its citizens surpassing that of people in the United States?

The answer lies in China's political system, its revolutionary history, and the leadership of the CPC – which is surely, by any reasonable measure, the most successful political party in history. Fundamentally, what defines modern China and provides the basis for its success is the socialist system. Power is exercised by, and on behalf of, the people, not a small group of people that own and deploy capital. In capitalist countries, the capitalist class is the ruling class and has political mechanisms in place that allow it to privilege its own interests over those of ordinary people.

The U.S. is a far richer country than China, having industrialized two centuries earlier and having built a global imperialist system via which it continues to accrue significant economic benefits. And yet the U.S. cannot guarantee its people the same fundamental human rights as people in China enjoy. There are hundreds of thousands of homeless people in the U.S.; there are millions of children living in poverty; there are tens of millions that lack access to healthcare. These problems are getting worse, not better, because the ruling class is unwilling or unable to deploy the enormous resources required to fix them. While life improves for the Chinese people, the people of the U.S., U.K. and many other countries are suffering under policies of neoliberal austerity.

Deng Xiaoping stated in 1987 that "only the socialist system can eradicate poverty." The class structure of the People's Republic of China means that the needs of the people are always prioritized. China was able to register major successes in the war on poverty because it mobilized hundreds of thousands of people nationwide to work with poor communities and identify means to sustainably and permanently improve their living conditions. As Xi Jinping has observed, "thanks to the sustained efforts of the Chinese people from generation to generation, those who once lived in poverty no longer have to worry about food or clothing or access to education, housing and medical insurance."

The pandemic provides another example of the relative effectiveness of different political systems. The U.S. has suffered over a million deaths from COVID-19. The U.K. has suffered nearly 200,000. Meanwhile China has suffered a little over 27,000 COVID-19 deaths, in spite its population being four times larger than that of the U.S., and 20 times larger than that of the U.K. China has been infinitely more successful in controlling the pandemic because it, from the beginning, mobilized enormous resources to the project of saving human life. In the West, the priority was to protect profit, to ensure economic business-as-usual. Most ironically, China was successful in saving human lives but the West was not successful in protecting profits. Because China acted quickly to prevent COVID-19 getting out of control, it was able to maintain economic growth while the West fell into recession.

The struggle against climate breakdown is also instructive. Although China is still a developing country, it has emerged as by far the global leader in the generation and use of renewable energy. Xi Jinping has underscored the concept of ecological civilization, putting environmental sustainability at the heart of Chinese policy-making and mandating that China should "never again seek economic growth at the cost of the environment." And in 2021, China committed to peaking carbon emissions by 2030 and realizing carbon neutrality by 2060, and has already developed systematic programs for reaching these goals.

Responsible for a third of all investment in new energy worldwide, China's innovations have served to massively reduce the cost of solar, wind and hydro power globally, to the point where they are now price-competitive with fossil fuels in many parts of the world. China's total renewable energy capacity is greater than the U.S., the EU, Japan and the U.K. combined. Around 99 percent of the world's electric buses are in China, along with 70 percent of the world's high-speed rail. Furthermore, its forest coverage has increased from 12 percent in the early 1980s to 23 percent today.

As with its commitment to poverty alleviation and suppressing COVID-19, China's resolute commitment to building an ecological civilization is a manifestation of its socialist system and the outstanding leadership of the CPC.

China's successes since the founding of the PRC, and the successes it will surely achieve on the path to becoming a great modern socialist country in all respects, will undoubtedly inspire progressive people the world over.